CHILDREN'S BIBLE

To my grand-children Carla-Esther and Fernan-do... and to all the children in the world, so that they may be initiated into the reading of the true written Word of God, and get the knowledge and wisdom en-closed in the Holy Books and, at the same time, be delighted by the illustrations, selected for their educa-tional value and executed in a clear and simple way, exclusively for them, in this children's Bible.

A. ORTELLS

Children's Bible

EDITORIAL ALFREDO ORTELLS, S. L.

NIHIL OBSTAT:
Rev. Fr. Antonio Cañizares Lloveras
Censor

IMPRIMI POTEST:
Very Rev. Fr. Juan Pérez Navarro
Vicar General

BY MANDATE OF:
Very Rev. Fr. Eduardo Tamarit Solbes
Chancellor-Secretary

Valencia, 3rd march 1989.

EDITORIAL DIRECTION:
Fernando J. Ortells González

TEXTS:
Rev. Fr. Samuel Valero Lorenzo

ENGLISH TRANSLATION:
Rev. Fr. Joseph G. Sáez

ILLUSTRATIONS:
Miguel Quesada Cerdán

© EDITORIAL ALFREDO ORTELLS, S.L.
C/. Sagunto, 5 - 46009 Valencia (España)

I.S.B.N.: 84-7189-390-8 (Mod. 1, Cartoné)
I.S.B.N.: 84-7189-391-6 (Mod. 2, Granoflex)
I.S.B.N.: 84-7189-392-4 (Mod. 3, Símil-piel)
I.S.B.N.: 84-7189-393-2 (Mod. 4, Símil-piel)
I.S.B.N.: 84-7189-394-0 (Mod. 5, Nacarina)

Depósito legal: M-38.672-2001

Impreso en Unigraf, S.L. (Madrid) - Printed in Spain.

To Parents

I have been walking through the city parks, those green spaces free of cement and asphalt. I have admired the gardens of some friend's country houses. I have also walked in rural areas and contemplated the wheat and barley fields.

In all three of these places I have seen the soil; soil cultivated, and cared for the eye's gratification or destined for food production.

However, in spite of the loving care of the gardener and the farmer, weeds are carried by the wind and fall in the same land.

What would happen to these lands without human work and effort? Unwanted weeds!

For the land produces what has been sown in it.

Your children are like the fertile land. Land cared for with love. The only thing needed is for the seed to fall on it, and certainly it will fall. If you don't do the sowing, the wind will.

Therefore, if you sow the good seed of the Word of God, even though weeds might appear, in the end the harvest will be good wheat to make the best bread.

Index

OLD TESTAMENT

NEW TESTAMENT

MAPS

16

Foreword

Before you start reading this book, you ought to have some information about the Bible.

God is its origin and author. Those men who have written it throughout many centuries have done it inspired by God, in such a way that they wrote, consciously or unconsciously, only what God wanted them to write. That's why the Bible is called «Word of God».

Of course the Bible is a religious book, by means of which God reveals fundamental and necessary truths for man in his relation with God in the present life, and also in his relation with other men; especially it reveals God's saving care over all of us.

The Bible is divided in two main parts: the Old and the New Testament. The Old Testament goes from the beginning of time to the coming of Jesus Christ to earth. The New Testament narrates the life of Christ and the story of the first disciples.

The Bible was written in Hebrew and Greek. The experts study it in its original languages. We read translations in our native tongues.

Both the Old and the New Testament consist of different parts called *books;* each book is made up of *chapters,* and the chapters likewise are divided into *verses.*

This Bible you are holding in your hands, has been shortened, adapted and illustrated for you to understand it better. Nevertheless, if you want to broaden your knowledge, you can see at the end of each chapter the quotations, in brackets, of the books from which the text has been taken.

May God lead you into reading the whole Bible when you grow up.

S. V. L.

Old Testament

The Creation

There was nothing. Besides God, there was nothing. Only God. And, just by willing it, out of love He started to make all the things that are.

From then on, the stars, plants and animals obeyed the laws He gave them, and for this reason, there was order in nature.

Only man and the angels were created with intelligence and freedom; with the power to choose. But only by choosing God could they be happy. And so they were, while they kept themselves faithful to the test God put them to.

Unfortunately they were led into temptation and disobeyed. After the sin of Adam and Eve, all the other sins followed and with them, all the evil things and disgraces.

As a good father, God wanted all the people to be his good children. In order to achieve this, sometimes He gave them good advice; other times punishment.

With Noah, God wanted to start again, but once more, people departed from their faith. God continued and still went on trying to make people happy with him.

Creation of the World

IN the beginning God created the heavens and the Earth. The Earth was formless wasteland and covered with darkness.

God wanted there to be light. And there was light. God then separated the light from darkness. God called the light «day» and the darkness «night».

Then He wanted there to be a firmament to separate the waters above from the waters below. And so it happened, and He called the firmament Heaven.

After that He wanted the waters under the firmament to gather together, so that the dry land would appear. It happened that way, and God called the dry land «the earth», and the joined waters «the sea». And he added: «Let the earth bring forth every kind of plant that produces seed and every fruit tree that produces fruit». And it happened that way.

Then God wanted there to be sun, moon and stars in the sky to separate the day from the night and govern the days, the seasons and the years. And so they appeared.

Then God created the fish, birds and all kinds of animals.

Finally, God said: «Let us make man in our image and likeness to have dominion over everything created». And He created man and woman.

(Genesis 1)

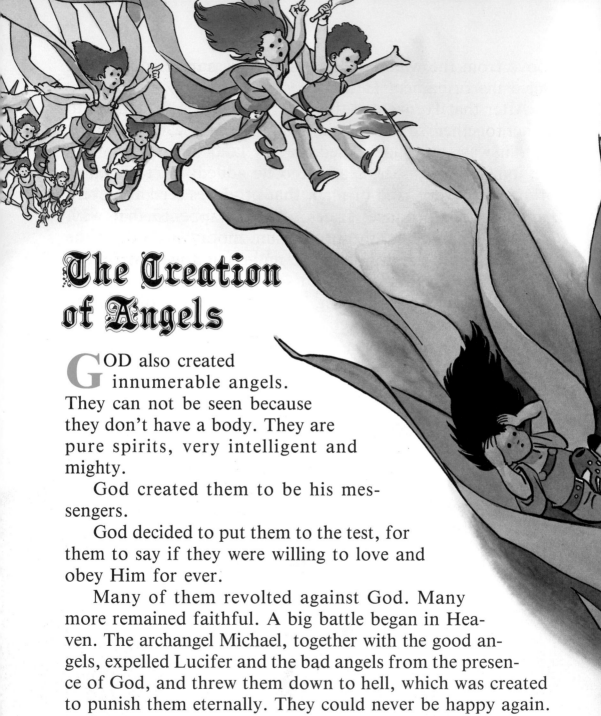

The Creation of Angels

GOD also created innumerable angels. They can not be seen because they don't have a body. They are pure spirits, very intelligent and mighty.

God created them to be his messengers.

God decided to put them to the test, for them to say if they were willing to love and obey Him for ever.

Many of them revolted against God. Many more remained faithful. A big battle began in Heaven. The archangel Michael, together with the good angels, expelled Lucifer and the bad angels from the presence of God, and threw them down to hell, which was created to punish them eternally. They could never be happy again.

But, the good angels remained for ever in Heaven contemplating the face of God, and ready to fulfill his orders.

When man appeared, the same battle as had happened in Heaven occurred on Earth. Lucifer, known as the Devil or Satan, and the fallen angels, also known as demons, tempted man into sin, so they would not go to Heaven and be happy. They did this because of hatred of God and envy of man. But God gave a guardian angel to every human being. He is man's ally in his battle against demons; he protects him from danger of body and soul, and helps him with good inspirations in the pathway to God.

We must ask for his help and be grateful for his services.

Paradise

GOD created Adam out of clay and blew into his nostrils the breath of life. He received a soul, and started his life with intelligence to know and free will to choose.

God placed him in a delightful garden, called Eden. It had rivers and trees for Adam to cultivate. In the middle of the garden there were two trees: the tree of life and the tree of the knowledge.

If he ate the fruit of the first one he would become immortal.

The fruit of the second one would cause him death. God gave Adam orders not to eat this fruit, and warned him:

—The day you eat this fruit you are doomed to die.

Adam was the first and only man on Earth. He enjoyed God's company and friendship. His body obeyed him without tiring. Whatever he did he never got tired. He enjoyed himself watching the animals and he gave them all a name. He was very happy and had everything he wanted at his disposal. He noticed that he didn't have anybody like him, and then he felt lonely.

God cured him of his loneliness. He cast Adam into a deep sleep, then took out one of his ribs, and with this he created a woman.

Adam was very happy with her presence and said:

—At last, this one is bone of my bones and flesh of my flesh.

Adam and the woman walked around naked without embarrassment. God would visit them and walk along with them in paradise. That's the way it was supposed to be until the day when God would take them to Heaven, without them going through the pain of death.

The tree of knowledge was still there, in the middle of the garden, to test their obedience to God.

(Genesis 2)

27

𝕿𝖍𝖊 𝕾𝖎𝖓 𝖔𝖋 𝕬𝖉𝖆𝖒 𝖆𝖓𝖉 𝕰𝖛𝖊

THE Devil started feeling envious of man. He talked to the woman when she was alone, through the cunning serpent.

—Is it true that God doesn't allow you to eat the fruit of all the trees?

—We may eat from all of them, except the one which is in the middle of the garden. He has told us that if we eat this fruit, we will die.

—You will not die! If you eat it you will be like God, knowing what is good and what is bad.

The woman, tricked by the serpent, took the fruit. It looked good. She ate it and gave some to Adam, who also tasted it.

They had just disobeyed.

They heard the sound of God walking about the garden and hid themselves. They could not stand his presence. They were ashamed of their nakedness and sin. When God questioned them they blamed each other: Adam blamed the woman and the woman the serpent. God cursed the three of them.

God gave them leather garments and banished them from the garden. At the gate He placed two cherubims with fiery swords to prevent them from returning. They would be unable to eat from the tree of life again.

Adam called his wife Eve, which meant mother of all men. They both were all mankind, and all human beings sinned with them. Thus, we all are born without the grace of God, subject to pain, fatigue and death. That sin sowed malice in the human heart.

(Genesis 3)

Cain and Abel

ADAM and Eve were sorry for their sin. They never forgot about God, but the seed of evil was already sown in man's heart.

They had sons and daughters. The two oldest were called Cain and Abel. Cain was a tiller of the soil, and Abel a shepherd.

Both offered sacrifices to God. Abel was generous and offered the best firstlings of his flock. This was looked on with favor and blessed by God. Cain, dominated by selfishness, would always offer the worst of his harvest, and God rejected his offerings.

Envy toward Abel was growing in Cain's heart. Deep in his soul he could hear the voice of God saying to him:

—Do well and you will be happy; but if not, sin is like a demon lurking at the door like a wild beast!

Cain was not willing to overcome his evil inclinations. One day, when they were together out in the fields, he attacked Abel and killed him.

This first murder cried out to heaven. God asked Cain:

—Where is your brother Abel?

—I don't know. Am I my brother's keeper?

Then Cain departed from God.

He fled from those lands and became a restless wanderer. Overcome by his crime, he feared that he might be killed by anyone; but God put a mark on him in case anyone should attempt to kill him. Eventually, he settled in the land of Nod with his wife.

Adam and Eve had another son. He was good-hearted like Abel, and they called him Set.

(Genesis 4)

The Flood

AFTER many years the human race had multiplied over the face of the earth. God saw how depraved men had become and He regretted that He had created them.

There was only one good man, Noah, and God said to him:

—The earth is full of lawlessness because of men; so I will destroy them.

And then, He explained to him how to build a very large ark of resin-wood, and cover it with pitch inside and out; something like a twin-decker ship.

When the ark was finished, God said to Noah to take all kinds of animals in pairs, a male and its mate; to take an abundant supply of provisions and go into the ark with his wife, his three sons, Shem, Ham and Japheth, and their wives.

For forty days and forty nights heavy rain poured on the earth and all living creatures from that region were wiped out.

(Genesis 6; 7)

Covenant between God and Noah

AFTER one hundred and fifty days, the waters of the flood began to subside, and the ark came to rest on the top of mount Ararat. Three months later the tops of the mountains appeared. The waters continued to diminish.

Noah opened the hatch he had made in the ark and he sent out a raven which started to fly back and forth, until one day it disappeared. Then he sent out a dove; it returned to the ark after a long flight. Noah thought it had returned because

the water prevented it from perching on the ground. After a
few more days he sent it out again. In the evening the dove
came back, and there in its beak was a plucked-off olive leaf.
Noah knew that was the sign that he could get out of the ark.

Noah removed the covering of the ark; he looked around
and saw that the surface of the ground was drying out. He
released all the animals and let them abound on the earth,
breeding and multiplying.

Noah built up an altar and he offered a sacrifice to God.
And God, with kind eyes, looked at those creatures which had
been spared, and He said to himself: «Never again will I
doom the Earth because of man, since the desires of man's
heart are evil from the start.»

Then He said to Noah and his children:

—Multiply and fill the Earth and subdue it. Every living
creature shall be yours to eat. Everything is yours; I give it
to you.

And He added:

—I am now establishing a covenant with you; there shall
not be another flood. My bow in the clouds is the sign of my
covenant.

At that moment the rainbow appeared. Noah and his family felt God's blessing upon them. Shem, Ham and Japhet
had many children and started to fill the Earth with people.

(Genesis 8; 9)

The Tower of Babel

SHEM'S descendants emigrated towards the East, and they settled in the land of Shinar. They discovered a beautiful valley and they decided to build a city there, and in the city, a tower with its top in the sky.

—With it we will become famous —they said to themselves.

They moulded bricks and tried to harden them with fire. This way they were able to make a material as hard as a rock.

And they started to build up the tower.

As the work was in progress, they would consider many different ways to build the tower, and very often there were arguments amongst the chiefs and the workers.

God saw that only pride and selfishness were moving those people to build such a grandiose structure, and He decided to humiliate them for their ridiculous pretension.

All of them spoke the same language. And God said:

—I am going to confuse their language so they will not understand each other.

And it happened that way. All were confused, misunderstood and disorganised. They just could not find a way to agree on anything.

They decided to scatter, leaving behind the unfinished tower.

It was the tower of Babel, so called because it means that God confused the tongues there.

(Genesis 11)

The Chosen People

Mankind is like a river. It starts on top of the mountains forming insignificant springs; some join others; they become big and, often overflow and make the low lands fertile.

God willed to choose such a river which would carry in its stream the salvation of mankind. This river happened to be «The Chosen People of God».

It all started with only one man, Abraham, some 1.850 years before Christ. God called him to be the beginning of the stream.

God revealed Himself to Abraham expecting his faith in return. Faith in God and in His promises; that he will possess the land of Canaan and, because of his numerous lineage, all nations will be blessed upon the face of the Earth.

From Abraham on, faith in the only and true God has been transmitted to the new People of God, which is the Church of Christ.

God governs the history of men to enable them to reach the goal He has prepared.

In Egypt, Abraham's lineage started to become a numerous nation.

Abraham's calling

ONCE again wickedness had taken over mankind. The true God had been almost completely forgotten. He had been replaced by idols.

In the city of Ur of the Chaldeans there was a pious man named Abram, married to Sarai. God said to him:

—Leave your country and your father's house, and go to the land I will show you.

And Abram, one day, left Haran with Sarai and his nephew Lot. He also took along with him many servants, his sheep and camels.

When he came to Canaan, God said to him:

—To your descendants I will give this land. You will be the father of a great nation, and because of you all nations will be blessed. No longer shall you be called Abram, but Abraham, for you will become the father of a host of nations. And for Sarai you shall call her Sarah for many rulers of peoples will be born of her. I shall be your God, and you my people. The People of God.

(Genesis 12, 13; 17, 1-16)

41

Melchizedek

THE rulers of the cities on the river Jordan banks were in disagreement, and ended in war. Sodom and Gomorrah fell to the hands of the conquerors. They ransacked them and took all their inhabitants as prisoners.

Lot, Abraham's nephew who dwelled in Sodom, was also taken prisoner. Someone who was able to escape gave Abraham the news about what had happened. Immediately he mobilized an army and defeated the foe.

When Abraham returned victorious, the king of Sodom, and Melchizedek, king of Salem, went out to pay him homage.

The king of Sodom told him to keep all the possessions he had recovered in the battle; but Abraham did not want to keep anything.

Melchizedek, king of Salem, was also a priest of God Most High, and brought out bread and

wine to be offered as a sacrifice. Whilst doing this he blessed Abraham by saying: «Blessed be by God Most High, the creator of heaven and earth.»

Abraham, in gratitude, gave him a tenth of the spoils.

(Genesis 14)

Sodom and Gomorrah

MANY atrocities were committed in Sodom and Gomorrah. One day God appeared to Abraham and said to him that He was going to destroy those two cities. Abraham begged God to be compassionate because there were at least fifty good people in those cities.

—I would not punish them if that was the case —God answered.

—And, in the case there were only forty?

—I would not punish them either.

Abraham kept insisting and bargaining until he reduced his demands to ten.

God said again:

—For the sake of those ten I would not destroy them.

Two messengers of God reached Sodom and from Lot's house they witnessed the abominable sins committed by those people. They said to Lot that he should leave quickly together with his wife and two daughters, and flee up to the hills, without looking back, or they would be turned into pillars of salt.

The sun was just rising when a sulphurous fire started falling down upon Sodom and Gomorrah. These two cities, with their inhabitants were destroyed. Lot's wife looked back and was turned into a pillar of salt.

(Genesis 18; 19)

God tests Abraham's faith

ABRAHAM and Sarah did not have children, and because they were old they could not have them. Nevertheless, God had announced to them that they would have many descendants.

Under the shade of Abraham's tent, God said to him that within a year Sarah would give him a son to be called Isaac. She was listening inside the tent and laughed.

After a year, indeed, Isaac was born, filling them with happiness. But, one day God gave Abraham a command:

—Take your son Isaac whom you love so much; go with him, and offer him in sacrifice up on the hill that I will point out to you.

Abraham must have been puzzled; but he obeyed.

They reached the place which God had indicated. Abraham built an altar, and arranged the wood on it; he tied up his son and placed him on the altar. He took the knife and, raising his arm, was ready to sacrifice him. At that moment, an angel of God stopped him, and said:

—Do not slaughter him! I know how God-fearing you are.

(Genesis 18, 9-15; 21, 1-7; 22)

47

Isaac and Rebekah

ONE day Abraham, being very old, called the oldest of his servants and gave him a very important task. He did not want his son Isaac to marry a woman from Canaan. Sarah had already passed away.

The old servant took with him ten camels loaded with rich presents and started his long journey to Chaldea. After many days of traveling he reached the city gates of Haran at sunset. He stopped the camels by the well, and waited for the towns-women to come out to draw water.

Then, a beautiful girl came out. She filled her jug and, when she was about to leave, the old servant asked her to give him a drink of water from the jug she had just filled. The girl, not only gave him water but she also started to fill the

drinking trough so that the camels could drink.

That girl was the chosen one. What she had just done was the sign the old servant had asked God for in order to recognize her.

—Tell me what is your name and whose daughter are you —he requested.

—I am Rebekah, the daughter of Bethuel, the son of Nahor —she answered.

The old man felt his heart beating fast. Nahor happened to be his master Abraham's brother, and therefore, Rebekah was Isaac's nicce. He presented her with a ring and two gold bracelets. Then the girl ran off and told her mother's household about it.

Her brother Laban rushed out to look for the old man, and invited him to stay at the house. He told them that, by orders of his master Abraham, he had come to get a wife for his son Isaac among the relatives of his father's house.

Rebekah and her family accepted his offer. Next day he took Rebekah and her maid and went on his way back home.

When Isaac saw Rebekah, he took her right away as his wife.

(Genesis 24)

Esau and Jacob

THE years passed and Rebekah brought
forth twins. Esau was the first-born and
then Jacob followed. The boys grew. Esau was hairy and Jacob smooth-skinned. The first one was preferred by his father
because he was fond of hunting and lived in the open, whereas Jacob kept to his tents, and his mother preferred him.

One day Jacob was cooking some lentil stew. Esau came
in from hunting famished, and said to him:

—I will give you my birthright in exchange for a bowl of
this lentil stew.

—Swear to me first! —said Jacob.

Esau swore; he gulped down the lentil stew, and sold his
birthright.

Isaac was getting so old that his eyesight had failed him.
The moment had arrived to relinquish all his rights to his
first-born son. He called Esau, and told him to go out into the
country to hunt some game and prepare a dish for him.

After eating he would give him his blessing. Rebekah, who had been listening, said to Jacob to bring her two kids from the flock. And quickly she cooked them. She dressed Jacob with Esau's best clothes, and covered up his arms with the skins of the kids. Then she sent him to serve the dish to his father, and be blessed before Esau would be back.

—Father, please, eat this I have just prepared for you —said Jacob.

—The voice is Jacob's. Come closer that I may feel you and make sure you are Esau.

The hairy arms, due to the skins of the kids and the fragrance of Esau's clothes, deceived Isaac. He ate and gave Jacob his blessing.

Then Esau came in with his dish. Although Isaac complained for being deceived, it was Jacob who became the heir by his father's blessing.

(Genesis 25, 9-34; 27)

Jacob's stairway

BEGRUDGED because of everything that had happened, Esau threatened to kill his brother, and, in order to prevent it, Rebekah asked Jacob to flee until Esau's fury would subside. Isaac advised him to take advantage of his journey and choose a wife from his mother's land, of his uncle Laban's house.

Jacob fled and proceeded toward Haran. At nightfall on the first day's journey he lay down on the ground and put a stone under his head to sleep there. He dreamed of a stairway which rested on the ground and reached to the heavens; angels of God were going up and down on it, and God, standing above, said to him:

—The land on which you are lying I will give you

and your descendants. I am with you; I will take care of you wherever you go. And bring you back to this land.

Jacob awoke full of wonder. He poured oil on the stone he had put under his head.

He kept walking for many days, when he saw some droves of sheep by a well. He asked the shepherds where they came from. They answered that they came from Haran. Then he asked them if they happened to know Laban. As a matter of fact they knew him, and pointing to a girl who was approaching the well with her flock, they said that she was Rachel, one of Laban's daughters. He introduced himself to Rachel and burst into years of joy for having met a relative of his.

He spent many years working for his uncle and finally he married Rachel. Then he returned to Canaan with great wealth.

When he arrived in Mambre he was able to embrace his aged father Isaac, who died shortly afterwards.

(Genesis 27, 41-46; 28; 29)

The sons of Jacob

GOD spoke to Jacob in Bethel and gave him a new name, Israel. God said that from him a nation would spring, an assembly of nations, and there would be kings among his descendants. And again He said that the land He once gave to Abraham and Isaac was given to him and his descendants.

They departed from that place, and shortly before they arrived in their new encampment, Rachel gave birth and died in the delivery. This new born child was given the name of Benjamin. The last of Jacob's sons. The others were born while he was at his uncle Laban's house. They were: Reuben, Simeon, Levi, Judah, Dan, Naphtali, Gad, Asher, Issachar, Zebulun and Joseph.

The twelve sons of Jacob would be the heads of the twelve tribes of the people of Israel.

(Genesis 35)

Joseph is sold by his brothers

JOSEPH was Jacob's favorite son, that's why his brothers were envious and jealous of him. One day he told them that he had a dream: There they were binding sheaves in the field and his sheaf rose to an upright position, whereas theirs gathered round it bowing down in adoration. In another dream, he told them that the Sun, the Moon and the stars were also bowing down to him. Jacob reprimanded Joseph for telling them those dreams, and, as predicted, his brothers' envy turned into hate. One day it happened that Joseph's brothers were pasturing their flocks far from home, and it had been a long time since Jacob had heard from them last, so he sent Joseph to see if all was well with them. They saw him approaching in the distance; they recognized him by the colorful tunic which used to belong to their father.

—Here comes that dreamer. Let us kill him and see what becomes of his dreams —they plotted.

Reuben, the eldest brother, intending to save his life, suggested to them to throw him into a dry cistern. They agreed. When Joseph came up to them, they stripped him of his tunic and threw him into the cistern.

Reuben went off to watch the flock and after awhile he came up to the well with the intention of rescuing Joseph and sending him back home, well and safe. But he was not there. Angry and saddened he returned to his brothers.

—What have you done to him? —he asked them.

They said that while they were having their meal they saw a caravan, and Judah thought it would be better to sell him as a slave instead of letting him die. And so they did, trading him for twenty silver coins to those merchants who were on their way to Egypt.

They sent to their father Jacob the tunic, stained with the blood of a goat, letting him believe that a wild beast had devoured him. Jacob mourned his son as dead, and only many years afterwards he would know the truth.

(Genesis 37)

Joseph and Pharaoh's dreams

THE merchants sold Joseph as soon as they arrived in Egypt, and the buyer was a chief of the pharaoh's escort. Because of his industry, uprightness and honesty, his master appointed him administrator of all his possessions.

Unfortunately, he became the victim of slander, and thrown into jail.

Two of his cell mates, who had previously been pharaoh's servants, told Joseph about some dreams they had had, and Joseph interpreted them, foretelling that they would get out of jail in a short time. A few days later both were free. One of them was pharaoh's chief cupbearer.

Time passed and one day they told Joseph the pharaoh requested his presence, because he had had a dream and none of his magicians could interpret it; then the cup-bearer, Joseph's former cell mate, thought of him.

Joseph shaved and changed his clothes, and then he was taken to the palace, and listened to the pharaoh's double dream. And he not only interpreted it, but also advised him what to do.

—The seven fat cows coming out of the Nile and the seven ears of grain, full and healthy, mean seven years in a row of abundant harvest. The seven thin cows and the seven empty ears mean another seven years of poor harvest and famine throughout the

Empire. My advice is that you appoint an intelligent and honest man to administer the country.

The pharaoh ordered him to take over the administration of Egypt.

Eventually he got married and had two sons, Manasseh and Ephraim.

(Genesis 39-41)

Joseph recognizes his brothers

THE years of famine, the time of the thin cows, also arrived in the land of Canaan. Jacob learned that there was plenty of wheat in Egypt, and he sent his sons to buy some. When they arrived there, Joseph recognized them, but they did not recognise Joseph. He pretended he was taking them as foreign spies and threatened to throw them into jail.

In order to avoid it, they told him where they came from and that also they had a younger brother who remained in Canaan with Jacob, their father. Joseph demanded that they should bring the younger brother they claimed to have. Simeon would remain as a hostage until they came back.

He allowed them to buy some wheat. When they arrived in Canaan they found out that the same money used to pay for the wheat, was inside the sacks.

Then, they went back together with Benjamin. They also brought with them the money they found in the sacks.

Joseph gave them a big banquet, and, secretly told his chief steward to put his silver cup inside Benjamin's sack, and also their money in the other sacks, as he did before.

They were on their way out of the city with the donkeys loaded, when the steward caught up with them. He searched the sacks and Joseph's cup appeared in Benjamin's.

They were brought back to Joseph. He spoke to them with severity and said that the thief would have to remain in jail.

Watching the expression on their faces, Joseph could not pretend any more, and crying with joy, embraced them, revealing who he was, and that they didn't have to worry about what they had done to him so many years back.

(Genesis 42-45)

The whole family migrates to Egypt

JOSEPH said goodbye to his brothers with a request to ask their father to leave Canaan and move with the whole family to Egypt. In order to facilitate the moving of family, belongings and flocks, he gave them wagons also. He reassured them that they would have fertile lands and pasture for their flocks.

Jacob felt immensely happy when his sons told him about their meeting with Joseph, and said:

—My son Joseph is still alive! We must go and I'll be able to embrace him before I die.

They organized a caravan and then started their journey. There were about seventy five people. Before they departed, Jacob offered sacrifices to find out if it really was God's will that they would leave Canaan. Then, he heard his voice saying:

—Jacob, do not be afraid to go down to Egypt. I will make you a great nation. I will go with you and bring you back.

Jacob sent Judah ahead to notify Joseph, who came out, riding his magnificent chariot, to meet his father. They embraced with tenderness and wept with joy.

Joseph introduced his father and brothers to the pharaoh, who said that the whole land of Egypt was at their disposal; that they could settle in Goshen, which happened to be the best land in the country.

Some time later Jacob died, and they took him to be buried in Canaan in fulfilment of a wish.

(Genesis 46-50)

Moses

JOSEPH died. Years and centuries passed. Pharaohs followed pharaohs. And the people of Israel were not receiving favours any longer. On the contrary. A pharaoh thought that such numerous descendants of that race could become a danger for Egypt.

64

For this reason he subjected the people of Israel to slavery; he forced them to do the hardest type of labour, and gave orders to kill the Israelites' sons at birth.

A woman from the tribe of Levi bore a son. He was goodly. She hid him for three months; but she could not keep him much longer without being discovered.

She fixed a basket, woven with rattan and papyrus, and putting her son in it, placed it among the reeds on the river bank. The child's sister was watching from the distance.

Pharaoh's daughter came down to the river to bathe and noticed the basket. She sent her handmaids to fetch it. On opening it she saw the baby boy who started to cry. She was moved with pity and thought he must be a Hebrew's child. Then, his sister got near and asked pharaoh's daughter:

—Do you want me to call one of the Hebrew women to nurse the baby for you?

—Yes, do so!

And the girl ran fast to notify her mother. Pharaoh's daughter asked her to nurse the child.

When the child grew, the woman brought him to pharaoh's daughter, who adopted him as her son. She called him Moses, which means drawn from the waters.

Moses kept growing, and was brought up in the court. When he had grown up, he visited his kinsmen and was sorry for the way they were treated. On one occasion, in order to defend an Israelite he slew an Egyptian. Moses became afraid and fled.

(Exodus 1; 2)

The burning bush

IN his flight Moses reached the desert of Midian, where he found refuge. And there he married a daughter of Jethro, and became a shepherd.

Meanwhile the king of Egypt died. The Israelites continued in their affliction under slavery, and their cries reached up to Heaven. God had present in his mind his covenant with Abraham, Isaac and Jacob.

Moses was tending the flock by the slopes of mount Horeb when he noticed the bright light of a burning bush which, in spite of this, was not consumed. A voice stopped him:

—Come no nearer and remove your sandals for the ground where you stand is holy!

Moses realized it was God who spoke to him. He hid his face with his hands and listened reverently:

—Go to the pharaoh for I want you to lead my people out of Egypt into the land of Canaan. I will be with you. Go and assemble the elders of Israel and tell them that the God of your fathers sends you.

—And, what if they don't believe me? —asked Moses.

God gave him the power to perform miracles with his staff, and so prove to his people and to the pharaoh that it was He who sent him. He also said that his brother Aaron would be his spokesman.

(Exodus 3; 4)

The ten plagues

MOSES and his brother Aaron explained, before the assembly of the elders, the plan God had conveyed to them. The people of Israel believed in them and regained hope of being free.

On the contrary, the first meeting with the pharaoh was a complete failure. He not only refused to let the people of Israel go, but forced upon them even harder labours. People blamed Moses for their misfortune, because he had confronted the pharaoh.

Moses complained to God, who told him to warn pharaoh about the calamities which would befall him if he didn't submit to his demands. Pharaoh didn't pay attention, and God began to act through Moses.

One day the waters of the Nile, its channels and ponds were stained with blood. After this, frogs covered and devastated the land. Some time later, mosquitoes multiplied like dust. Later, a plague of gnats made life miserable for all the people.

Confronted with

such calamities, it seemed like the pharaoh was going to give in. Moses, using his power, stopped the plague, but, once again the king's heart hardened, and he refused once more.

Another plague befell and decimated the livestock of the Egyptians and men were covered with pestilent ulcers. The pharaoh went on stubbornly refusing. A hailstorm destroyed the crops, and a plague of locusts completely ravaged the fields.

At each calamity the pharaoh would call Moses and give him permission for the people of Israel to leave; but, when Moses had finished with the plague, he would deny permission again.

The last punishment was going to be terrible, and the pharaoh would be forced to yield.

(Exodus 5-10)

69

The Exodus from Egypt

THE pharaoh kept on in his negative attitude, and Moses for the last time, and as a divine spokesman, said to him:
—At midnight every firstborn in Egypt will die, from the crown prince to the most humble of the slaves, as well as the

firstlings of the flocks. The children of Israel will not be hurt. Your people will beg me to depart from Egypt, and only then we will leave.

Moses had given the Israelites instructions about what they were supposed to do that night: Each family would sacrifice a lamb, and with its blood sprinkle the lintel and the two doorposts; no one should go outside; they should roast the sacrificed animal and eat it, standing on their feet, with everything ready to initiate their departure from Egypt.

The mark on the doors would be the signal that God would not strike any of their dwellers.

At midnight death visited the houses of all the Egyptians.

There was no family that would not wail for a dead one. The Egyptians were horrified and begged the Israelites to leave. The pharaoh summoned Moses and his brother and told them to leave Egypt, together with all the people of Israel.

(Exodus 11-13)

Crossing of the Red Sea

IN battle array the Israelites marched out of Egypt, and camp-
ed near the edge of the desert. A cloud in the shape of
a column protected them under its shadow during day time,
and gave them light during the night. It was the protective
presence of God, extended over the Israelites. With two more
day's journey they arrived at the shores of the Red Sea.

The pharaoh realized he had let go a whole population of
slaves, who rendered him important services; so, he changed
his mind and decided to catch up with them and force them
to return to Egypt.

He led an army of
six hundred chariots
with his best charioteers.
The pursuit was initiated at
high speed. The roar and the
dust cloud raised by the chariots
could be noticed from a distance in the
desert.

The israelites saw them advance and they were
overcome by fear. They had some weapons but
they were not expert warriors. They cried
out to God, and complained to Moses

for having led them out to die in the desert, since the Red Sea prevented them from going on with their flight.

Moses told them not to fear and be calm and that they would see immediately the wondrous way they would be saved. He stretched out his hand and a strong wind started to blow, splitting the sea in two, separating the waters, and leaving a dry passage. The Israelites were able to pass through.

The pharaoh's army followed in pursuit right into the dry bottom of the sea. When the Israelites had finished going through to the other side, Moses stretched out his hand again, the wind stopped and the waters returned to their previous level and the pharaoh and all his warriors, charioteers and horses perished.

The people of Israel witnessed the whole thing from the other side of the Red Sea, and then, Moses and the Israelites sang a triumphant hymn to Almighty God.

(Exodus 14)

Towards Sinai

THEY had spent several months going through the desert. Food and water became scarce, and they missed the meat and bread from Egypt, without remembering they had eaten them while they were submitted to slavery. And they started grumbling about Moses and Aaron.

God came forward to help them once again, and told them that that very same evening they would eat meat, and the following morning they would have bread. An enormous flock of quail came up and covered the camp, and they were able to eat meat that evening. In the morning a dew lay all about the camp, and when the dew evaporated there were fine flakes which tasted just like bread.

—«*Man-ha?*» (What is this?) —they asked.

—This is the bread which the Lord has given you to eat —said Moses.

Whilst they crossed the desert, the Israelites gathered this divine food or «man-ha» each morning, but only as much as they needed for a day's journey.

Encampment after

encampment, from oasis to oasis, the people were getting closer and closer to the Sinai mountains. In the evenings, when they rested, Moses would sit down to listen to and solve the quarrels arising among the people.

One day Amalek and his people attacked the Israelites. Next morning, and by orders from Moses, Joshua went out at the head of a group of men to fight the Amalekites. Moses climbed to the top of a hill to pray for his people's victory. As long as Moses kept his hands raised, Joshua had the better of the fight, but when he let his hands rest, Amalek had the better of the fight. His companions, Aaron and a messenger, noticed this circumstance and supported his arms, until the Amalekites were completely defeated. It was at the end of the third month since their escape from Egypt, when the Israelites reached the slopes of mount Sinai.

God told Moses to come up to the top of the mountain because He wanted to speak to him.

(Exodus 16; 17)

The Ten Commandments

WHEN Moses was at the top of Mount Sinai, God let him know his message for him to transmit to the people:

—If you hearken to my voice and keep my covenant, you shall be my people and I shall make you a holy nation.

When the people heard what God intended, they answered:

—Everything the Lord said, we will do!

Early in the morning there were peals of thunder and lightning, a heavy and dark cloud covered the mountain in which could be heard, within the rumble of thunders, a very loud trumpet blast. God summoned Moses to go through the cloud to the top of the mountain.

Moses recorded in the Book of the Covenant everything God had said to him. Then he erected an altar and they sacrificed several young bulls. Then he read what was written in the Book of the Covenant, and the people answered:

—All that the Lord has said, we will heed and do!

Then Moses took the blood of the young bulls and sprinkled it on the people and the Book, saying:

—This is the blood of the Covenant which the Lord has made with you in accordance with all these words of his.

This way the Covenant between God and the people of Israel was sealed.

(Exodus 19; 20; 24, 3-8)

The golden calf

ONCE again God summoned Moses to the top of Mount Sinai. Moses stayed there for forty days and nights, receiving more detailed explanations about the Ten Commandments. God also gave him civil laws to govern the people; He established holy days and all the necessary things for worship; He even dictated how the priestly vestments should be.

He instructed him how to build a portable temple, with fabrics hanging on frames.

He told him that the Ark of the Covenant had to be made of acacia wood, plated with gold, in which he would put the Book of the Covenant and the two stone tablets He was going to give him; how the seven branch lampstand had to be; the Altar of Holocausts; dimensions of the temple, etc.

The people got tired of waiting at the slopes of the hill and they thought that Moses would not return. They felt forsaken by him and by God. They spoke to Aaron and decided to make a God for themselves, like other peoples had done.

Everyone brought their earrings, coins and other golden objects; they melted everything and made a molten calf, and they worshiped it.

—This is the God who brought us out of Egypt! —they cried out, dancing around the altar they had erected.

When Moses came down the mountain with the two tablets on which the Decalogue was engraved, he found out what was happening, and, in anger, he threw the tablets down and ground the golden calf down to powder, which he scattered on the water and made the Israelites drink.

God's wrath flared up when He saw that they had broken the Covenant, to the point that he was ready to destroy them; but Moses implored the Lord to be patient and merciful with his people.

(Exodus 24, 12-18; 25; 32)

The wandering people

MOSES appeased the wrath of God, on account of the golden calf. Again he climbed the Sinai, ready with the two stone tablets, and came back with them engraved by the hand of God.

The people, sorry for their sin, shared in the construction of the portable temple. On the feast of the dedication, Moses invested and annointed Aaron as High Priest; and the cloud, symbol of God's presence, came down covering the temple.

The people of Israel remained on the slopes of the Sinai for about two years. Then, God ordered that the temple be taken down and the encampment removed, in order to resume their journey.

From encampment to encampment they went forward through the desert. If the cloud settled down over the temple, the encampment would not move forward; whenever the cloud rose from dwelling, the Israelites would set out on their journey.

The hard conditions of the desert were causing unhappiness among the people. Complaints against Moses became frequent. God felt offended on account of this, and some times He would punish them; other times He would favor them with miracles.

At one of the encampments, they found themselves without water. The people gathered and asked Moses and Aaron:

—Why have you led the Lord's chosen people to the desert for us and our flocks to perish? Why did you make us leave Egypt and bring us to this inhospitable land where nothing can be sown, without even water to drink?

Moses cried to the Lord. Then the Lord said to him:
—Strike a rock with your staff and water will spring up,
for all the people as well as their flocks to drink.
And Moses, fulfilling the will of God, did so and all
all the people could quench their thirst.

(Exodus 34; 35; 40; Numbers 16; 20)

Death of Moses

THEY were getting close to the Promised Land. The people of Israel were by then a renewed population, born and raised in the desert. Most of those who had come out of Egypt were dead. And all of them had died before entering the land of Canaan, except Joshua. Neither Moses nor Aaron would escape from this decision taken by God, as a punishment for their lack of faith, idolatry and other sins committed by the people.

God invited Moses to contemplate, from the top of a hill, the land He had promised to give to the descendants of Israel.

—After you see it, you will die, as your brother Aaron has already died —He said.

In effect, some years had passed since Aaron had died, near Mount Hor. His son Eleazar took up the functions of High Priest.

Moses, facing his death, asked God to appoint a man of strong spirit to lead his people. God told him to go down to the encampment and lay his hand on Joshua, and then present

him to the priest Elea-
zar and to the whole
community, and give
him his task.

Moses did as he
was told. Then he
said goodbye, after
reminding the people
of Israel of the
greatness of the
power of God,
and the ho-
nor bestow-
ed upon
them of

the punishments they would receive if they were not faithful
to a God so holy and mighty. He finished by giving his blessing to each one of the tribes of Israel.

Then, he climbed alone to the top of mount Nebo, and
from there he contemplated the valley of Jordan down below,
and Palestine, the Promised Land, in the distance; and, up
there he died. No one ever learned where he was buried.

(Numbers 20; 27; Deuteronomy 32-34)

Joshua

DURING Moses' time, the Israelites had conquered most of the cities located east of Jordan.

The fame of the mighty God who led them, had reached the other bank of the river.

Joshua sent two spies to reconnoiter the land and Jericho's defenses, and report back to him. After fording the river they got into the city, and lodged at the inn of a woman named Rahab. Jericho's guardians detected the presence of the two Israelites, and they started to search for them in order to capture them. Rahab hid them on the roof of the house among her stalks of flax. She said to the guards that the two men had been at her house, but they had left, at dark.

When the pursuers had left, Rahab came to them and said that the town was overcome with fear because they knew the God of the Israelites had given them the land of Canaan. Then she asked them to spare her life and that of her family, in return for her kindness, when they conquered the city.

The inn was built against the city wall and had a window going all the way through the wall. At dark, Rahab helped

the spies go down the wall with a rope. They said to her «put a scarlet cord in the window as a signal for the attackers, in order to spare the lives of those living in the house».

Back in the encampment they came to Joshua and reported all that had befallen them. The report was highly optimistic:

«All the inhabitants of the land are overcome with fear and they will not oppose any resistance to our attack».

(Numbers 21, 21-35; 32; Joshua 1-2)

The fall of Jericho

A few days later, the Israelites moved the encampment from Shittim to undertake the final march towards Jericho. In order to accomplish this task they had to cross over the river Jordan. They remained in expectancy for three days at the edge of the river. Finally the orders arrived and the priests carried the Ark of the Covenant on their shoulders, and waded into the waters. Immediately, the waters flowing from upstream halted. The priests remained motionless on dry ground until the whole nation had completed the passage. The Ark of the Lord was carried across the river and, then, the Jordan resumed its course.

Facing the arrival of the Israelites, the people of Jericho enclosed themselves within the walls, and from their vantage point, they watched the approaching Israelites. The people of Israel circled the city marching around it and, then, they returned to their encampment. They did this for six days.

On the seventh day at sunrise and in silence, they marched around the city again and again, before the astonished guards on the walls. On the seventh round Joshua gave the order:
—Now shout, for the Lord has given you the city!

The horns blew and the people, inflaamed with fervour raised a tremendous shout. The ground trembled and the walls collapsed. They stormed the city and put to the sword all its inhabitants, except Rahab and her family who were spared on account of the pledge made by the two Israelite spies.

(Joshua 3; 4; 6)

The conquest of the Promised Land continues

JOSHUA ordered three thousand of his men to conquer Ai city, since, according to the spies' reports, that many would be enough; but they returned defeated with many casualties. Joshua was puzzled; he turned to God who told him He had ordered that no one could take anything as his own in the conquest of Jericho, and that there wouldn't be any robbery or looting. But someone stole silver and gold. As a punishment for such disobedience, God had permitted their defeat in Ai. When they discovered the thief, he was stoned by the people.

A new expedition was organized and Joshua ordered a wing of the army to attack at dark at the northern part of the city. Joshua led the rest of the army advancing from the south. Immediately, the besieged ones came out to engage them in battle. Joshua, following his own plans, fled in seeming defeat and was pursued by the enemy. It was at that moment when the men in the north assaulted and burnt the city. When Joshua saw the columns of smoke from the distance he turned around and counter-attacked, and the men of Ai were hemmed in by the Israelites on either side, who thus gained a total victory.

Five kings of small kingdoms west of the Jordan all formed an alliance to launch an attack against Gibeon for having made a pact with the Israelites; but they were promptly defeated by Joshua. With this victory he had conquered a big share of the Promised Land.

(Joshua 7-10)

Gideon

AFTER more than forty years of their wandering through the desert, it wasn't easy for the Israelites to adjust themselves to the sedentary city life. They had to learn new trades, as well as new farming techniques.

Each time the Israelites were subjugated by their enemies, they were disheartened and they would go back to God begging his help; and God would provide his help by means of some humble warrior, chosen to lead the people. They were the so called judges.

One of these judges was Gideon.

Even though at the beginning he resisted God's call, he finally agreed to combat the Midianites, who were ruining the crops of the Israelites. Then he recruited a big army. So big that God told him to reduce it down to three hundred warriors.

—I want this to be clear, victory will be mine, not yours —God said.

At dark they surrounded the enemy encampment, and each one of the warriors was provided with a horn and an empty jar with a burning torch inside, so the light couldn't be seen. When Gideon gave the signal they broke the jars and blew the horns, and lifted the torches at the same time. The Midianites woke up terrified by the roar, and confused by the flashing torches. Such a chaos was created that they attacked themselves and fled in all directions.

The Midianites never again bothered the people of Israel.

(Judges 7; 8)

Samson

FOR their lack of faith, the Israelites fell into the power of the Philistines; then God appointed Samson to fight against them. He possessed extraordinary physical strength.

On one occasion he burnt all their crops tying burning torches to foxes' tails and letting them loose in the fields. The Philistines found out who did it; then they came out searching for him in order to kill him. But Samson attacked them with the jawbone of an ass as a weapon, and slayed over a thousand men.

Delilah, his wife, a Philistine herself, betrayed him, and when she found out that the source of his strength was his long hair, she waited for him to be asleep to shave it off, and used this way to destroy his strength.

The Philistines seized him easily and in revenge they gouged out his eyes, and condemned him to push a mill grinding stone.

Sometime later the Philistines assembled to offer a great sacrifice to their god Dagon and make merry. In order to be amused by Samson they brought him into the temple. He tricked his guards into placing him between the two columns that supported the building and he asked God to give him back his strength. With a great effort he pushed hard and said:

—Let me die with the Philistines!

The temple fell upon the people who were in it, and crushed them all. And thus Samson died.

(Judges 13-16)

Ruth

DURING the long era of the judges, there were years of famine. Elimelech with his wife Naomi, their two sons and the rest of the family, departed to reside on the plateau of Moab. The two sons married Moabite women, Orpah and Ruth. Elimelech died, and some years later his sons died also, leaving the three women widowed.

Naomi said to her daughters-in-law that she was returning to her parent's land; and for them to find new husbands and be happy again.

Orpah wept, kissed her mother-in-law good-by and departed.

But Ruth begged Naomi to let her stay: —Wherever you go I will go; do not ask me to forsake you. Your people shall be my people, and your God my God —she pledged.

They reached Bethlehem at harvest time. They were poor and Ruth, in order to survive, had to go to the fields and glean ears of grain after the harvesters.

Boaz was the owner of the fields where Ruth was gleaning the ears of barley that the harvesters were leaving behind. When he was approaching the fields to oversee the harvest, he saw the girl gleaning the ears of grain without rest, and he asked the overseer about her. He said she was Naomi's daughter-in-law who just had arrived in Moab. Boaz told her that she could glean in his fields and drink water from his workers' jars. He invited her to eat and, when she was ready to continue gleaning, Boaz also told his servants to drop some ears of grain for her. When Ruth went home she told Naomi everything; she was delighted because Boaz was her closest relative and he could take Ruth for his wife.

Boaz married her, attracted by her good sentiments. Ruth gave birth to Obed who was king David's grandfather.

(Ruth 1-4)

Samuel's calling

HANNAH didn't have children, and she prayed to God, weeping copiously, begging the favour to bear a son. She made the vow to give him to the service of the temple. Shortly afterwards, Samuel was born.

In those days the judge and High Priest of Israel was Eli. He lived in Shiloh, for it was there where the Ark of the Covenant was kept. His sons helped him in the temple; but they were wicked and commited many abuses in the service of God and against the people.

When Samuel was able to walk, Hannah took him to Eli, who accepted him to his service.

One night, while he was sleeping, he heard a voice calling his name:

—Samuel! Samuel!

—Here I am, Lord! —he answered, running to Eli. But Eli said he hadn't called him, and to go back to sleep. The same thing happened three times; the third time, Eli understood that the Lord was calling the youth, so he told him how to answer. When Samuel heard his name called again, he answered:

—Speak, Lord, for your servant is listening.

And God revealed the kind of punishments He was going to inflict upon the house of Eli, on account of his sons' wicked deeds. In the morning, Samuel, told Eli everything, and he accepted God's will.

The Philistines gathered their troops to attack Israel; then, the Council of the Elders asked for the Ark of the Covenant to be taken to the battlefield, so God would give them victory. The two sons of Eli carried the Ark all through the battle, but they were killed, as well as so many others, in a disastrous defeat. And the Ark was captured by the Philistines. When Eli heard the news of his sons' death, he suffered such a shock that he fell backward and died. Thus it was fulfilled what Samuel had prophesied.

After seven months, the Philistines returned the Ark of the Covenant because it was causing many afflictions upon their cities.

(I Samuel 1-6)

Samuel, the last of the Judges

THE Israelites thought they could defeat the Philistines in the next battles, because they had recovered the Ark of the Covenant. But, twenty years later they still hadn't been able to win. Samuel spoke to the people to show them what was the cause of their defeat.

—Put away all foreign gods and idols, and devote yourselves to God with all your hearts. Only this way you will get rid of the Philistines.

Inspired by Samuel, the people gathered at Mizpah to do penance, fasting and praying. The Philistines learned about this gathering and they mobilized their army to attack the Israelites by surprise. Hearing this, the Israelites became afraid and begged Samuel to implore the Lord unceasingly for them. While Samuel was offering the sacrifice, a big storm broke out, with lightning and loud thunder, and the Philistines were scared away. The Israelites pursued them all the way to victory, the first one in many years.

During Samuel's lifetime, many cities were recovered, and a long period of peace was enjoyed by all. When he grew old, he thought it was time for his two sons to succeed him as judges. But the elders of Israel came to him and said they didn't accept his sons; what they wanted was for Samuel to appoint

a king over them, as
other nations had. Sa-
muel was displeased by this
idea, for only God was the king of
Israel. The elders insisted. So, Samuel went to God who said to him:
«Grant their request». Samuel asked them for some time to think
about it.

A few days later he gathered the
people at Mizpah, and introduced
the king to them. He was handsome
and tall. Then, all the people shouted: «Long live the king!».

Samuel relinquished all his
functions as judge, and
reminded the people
that God was above
the king.

(I Samuel 7; 8; 12)

Saul, the first King

NOW the asses of Saul's father had wandered off; Saul was hunting for them when he met Samuel.

God manifested to Samuel that this man was the chosen one to be the king. Samuel invited him to his house and explained God's plan. Then, taking a flask of holy oil, anointed him as a king.

Saul didn't consider himself worthy nor able to rule his people. Reluctantly he was presented to the people of Mizpah; then he hid himself in his house, not showing any interest for the kingship.

Four months later the Ammonites laid siege to Jabeh-Gilead, with ignominious threats. They notified Saul when on his way home from the fields behind his oxen. He became very angry, and being aware he was the king, he called every able man to war. Three hundred thousand men placed themselves under his command; then, they attacked the Ammonites by surprise, killing many and dispersing the rest.

The whole of Israel became enthusiastic with their king. Samuel summoned the people at Gilgar where Saul was crowned in God's presence.

On one occasion, Saul offered the sacrifice as if he was the High Priest. Samuel became indignant for what the king had dared to do, and prophesied that his dynasty should not endure.

Saul fought all his enemies and always won. God ordered him, through Samuel, to destroy the Amalekites without sparing any one, neither taking spoils. The attack was victorious; but Saul spared king Agag's life, and took for himself the best of the cattle and spoils. It was then that Saul was reproved by God.

(I Samuel 9-11; 13; 15)

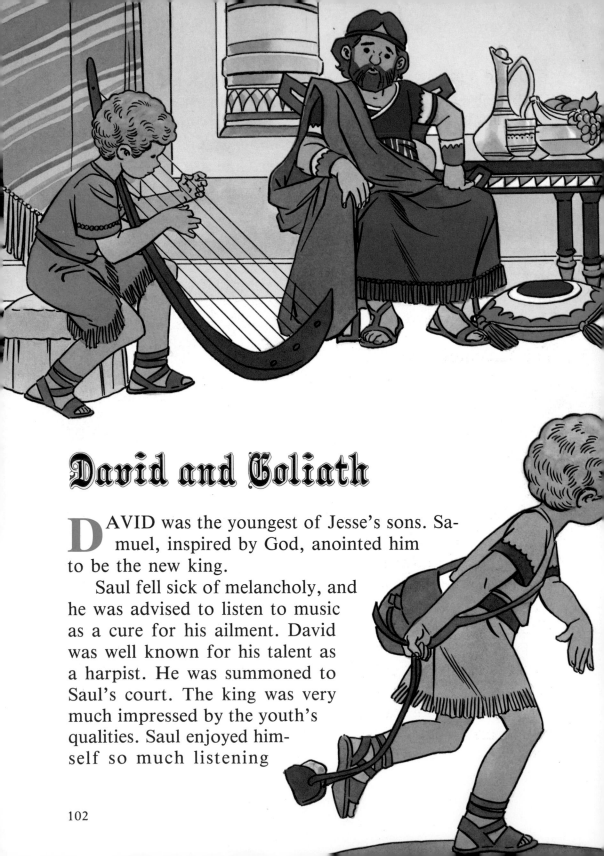

David and Goliath

DAVID was the youngest of Jesse's sons. Samuel, inspired by God, anointed him to be the new king.

Saul fell sick of melancholy, and he was advised to listen to music as a cure for his ailment. David was well known for his talent as a harpist. He was summoned to Saul's court. The king was very much impressed by the youth's qualities. Saul enjoyed himself so much listening to David's music that he made him his armorbearer.

The Philistines rallied their forces to attack Israel. Both armies were posted face to face. A gigantic champion from the Philistine camp came out and challenged any Israelite to fight against him. The Israelites were

dismayed and terror-stricken, but David convinced king Saul to let him come out. He took his shepherd's staff; he put five smooth stones from the wadi into his shepherd's bag and, with sling also ready to hand, he approached Goliath. When David was close enough, he put a stone in the sling; he hurled it and Goliath fell prostrate on the ground. He had been struck on his forehead. David ran and, with Goliath's own sword, cut off his head. The Philistine army disbanded. Saul went in pursuit of them and won a new victory.

David became famous. Jonathan, Saul's oldest son, took him as his best friend and put him in command of part of his army.

(I Samuel 16; 17; 18, 1-5)

Saul's jealousy

DAVID became very popular on account of his military victories. Each time he returned from battle against the Philistines, women welcomed him singing and dancing. All this irritated Saul who became so jealous of David that he attempted to kill him. On two occasions, while David was playing the harp to relieve his melancholy, Saul threw his spear to pierce him right through; but David avoided the blow both times and, finally, he fled from his presence.

David met his friend Jonathan and told him everything. Jonathan pledged to plead on his behalf before his father and that he would let David know about Saul's intentions. On the feast of the new chiefs, Abner and Jonathan were present too, but David was missing. Saul inquired about his absence, so Jonathan tried to excuse him. Saul became extremely angry and ordered his son to look for him, for he was doomed. Next morning Jonathan warned David, so he could flee and hide.

David became a wanderer, hiding in the cities and in the desert. His brothers and a number of discontented people and those who were in difficulties joined him. David became the leader of that group of about four hundred men; he fought some times against the Philistines and the Amalekites; on other occasions he had to make a pact with them in order to hide.

Saul, as soon as he heard of David's whereabouts, organised expeditions to kill him, but David always was able to slip away. On two occasions David was very close to Saul; on one of them, he took away his spear when he was inside his own tent. David could have killed Saul, but he didn't because he was his king.

Saul and Jonathan died fighting against the Philistines.

(I Samuel 18-31)

David reigns in Jerusalem

DAVID mourned over the deaths of Saul and Jonathan; then he went up to Hebron where he was anointed king of Judah. During seven years there were fights between David's followers and those of Ishbaal's, Saul's youngest son, whom Abner had made king of the other tribes, by means of his military power. But Abner eventually became convinced that David was God's chosen king, and then he gave up his plans for the sake of unity.

The Jebusites were proud of themselves and felt safe within Jerusalem's invulnerable walls. But David had chosen this city to be the nation's capital. He conquered it and established his dwelling place, and the seat of the government in it. Later he brought the Ark of the Covenant to the tent he had readied for it. Thus Jerusalem became also the center of worship for the people of Israel, the holy city of God.

After many years of warfare, the power of the Philistines was swept away, and peace was pacted with neighbouring nations. With David, the covenant promised to Abraham many centuries before was fulfilled: that Canaan would become the Chosen People's land.

David was an honest man; always faithful to God's will; but, unfortunately he also committed a big sin. He ordered that a general of his army be stationed at the most dangerous position in the fighting line, and thus be killed in battle; this way, his wife, with whom David was very much in love, would be widowed. David afterwards wept and paid for his sin.

Absalom, David's most loved son, organized a civil war declaring himself king of Hebron, moved by his own pride and by ill advice. Some time later, David's army defeated Absalom's henchmen. Absalom fled riding a mule, but he met his death when his long hair caught fast in the branches of a terebinth as he passed under this tree. The spear bearers who were after him, pierced him through.

(II Samuel 2; 5-18)

107

Solomon

DAVID was an old and sick man. So, he decided that his son, Solomon, be anointed king and be seated on his throne. David gave him good advice and shortly after he died. Solomon strengthened his throne and took in marriage the pharaoh of Egypt's daughter. Because of this marriage, Israel gained fame and respect among the other nations.

God had given Solomon great wisdom. One day two women who lived together, came before him. One of them was carrying a dead child in her arms, the other a living one. Both of them claimed the living child as her own. After listening to them, Solomon ordered a soldier to cut the child in two with his sword, and to give half of it to each one. One of the women fell to her knees before the king begging of him:

—Please, my lord, give her the living child, do not kill it.

This way Salomon found out which one of the two was the real mother of the child.

With his enormous wealth he built a magnificent palace, and, above all, he built the temple. When it was finished he summoned the people of Israel to carry the Ark of the

Covenant to its permanent place.
Solomon came to a bad end.
He departed from God's commandments, and even more, he
built temples to pagan gods. God
took away his blessings from the
king, and Israel's national unity
was broken.

(I Kings 1; 3; 6; 7; 8; 11)

Secession of Israel

JEROBOAM was an honest and brave man; that's why Solomon appointed him chief of his personal guard. One day it was prophesied that Solomon's kingdom would be split in two as a punishment for his idolatry, and that

Jeroboam would reign over ten tribes. Later on he had to flee to Egypt.

Solomon died and his son Rehoboam went to Sechem where the people would proclaim him king. After his coronation, Jeroboam, who had been summoned to the ceremony, as well as the whole people, petitioned the new king to mitigate the servitude, that they had been subjected to by his father; but he answered in a harsh manner, following the advice of his young counselors.

Because of so much injustice the people revolted and proclaimed Jeroboam as their king, in Sechem. Ten tribes followed him from the north, thus fulfilling the prophecy.

In Jerusalem the small tribes of Benjamin and Judah were faithful to Rehoboam. They organized an army to fight against their brother Israelites and this way rebuild the unity. They gave up because a prophet told them that such a division was brought about by God.

Jeroboam fortified Sechem to reign from there, building two temples to compete against the grandiose temple of Jerusalem, one in Bethel and the other in Dan. They established idolatry, worshipping a bull shaped statue in place of the true God. One day while Jeroboam was burning incense on the altar of Bethel a messenger of God arrived crying out that a descendant of David would sacrifice all the priests on such an altar. Then the altar broke up and the ashes strewed about. That was the sign that the Lord had spoken of.

The kingdom of Israel, which lasted for two hundred and fifty years, ended with Hoshea. During his reign the king of Assyria, Shalmaneser, conquered Samaria, enslaved all its inhabitants, and colonized it with people from other lands.

(I Kings 11, 28-40; 12; 13, 1-5; II Kings 17)

Elijah

DURING the years of Ahab and Ahaziah, kings of Israel, God spoke through the prophet Elijah. Ahab had offended God more than any previous king, and Elijah came to him to announce that there would be no rain for several years, as a punishment.

Ahab had given his consent for his wife Jezebel to order the slaughter of all the prophets of Israel. Elijah had to flee and hide in the gorge of a torrent at the other side of the Jordan. Ravens would bring bread and meat to feed him.

After three years God sent Elijah to Ahab because He was going to send rain. In order to show who the real God was, Elijah proposed that a bull be given to the priests of Baal and another to him; that they would prepare altars with wood but, without fire, at Mount Carmel, and

the bulls cut into pieces on top. The god who would respond with fire to ignite the wood would be the true God.'

The priests of Baal prepared everything and started singing and dancing around the altar, calling on their god.

—Call louder, perhaps Baal is asleep! —Elijah taunted them.

At the end they were exhausted, with no results.

Then Elijah repaired, with twelve stones, the altar of God that had been destroyed; he arranged the wood and placed the flesh of the bull on top. He ordered that jars of water be poured over the holocaust. Then he called on God and fire came down from the sky, and consumed everything.

All the people fell prostrate and said:

—This is the true God!

And they seized and killed the priests of Baal.

(I Kings 17; 18, 1-30)

The flaming chariot

ONE day, while Ahab was eating, Elijah climbed to the top of Carmel. He directed his servant to look out to sea while he was praying. After a while the servant said he could see a small cloud in the distance. Elijah told him to advise Ahab to leave before the rain stopped him. Shortly afterwards the sky grew dark with clouds and wind, and heavy rain fell.

Jezebel, Ahab's wife, learned about the slaughter of the priests of Baal and swore to kill Elijah. Once again Elijah

had to flee towards the desert, and, miraculously fed, he had the strength to reach the mount of Horeb. He stayed in a cave until God spoke to him. He sent him to Damascus where he would anoint the king of Syria and the king of Israel, and look for Elisha to be his successor as prophet. On his way, Elijah came upon Elisha as he was ploughing; then Elijah threw his cloak over him. Elisha left the oxen and ran after Elijah, and followed him as his attendant.

Elijah accomplished many other services that God dictated to him, and then he left Jericho; he miraculously crossed the Jordan together with Elisha. As they were on their way, a horse drawn flaming chariot came by; Elijah climbed into the chariot and went up to heaven in a whirlwind of fire.

(I Kings 18, 30-46; 19; II Kings 2)

Elisha

WHEN Elijah was taken up to heaven in the flaming chariot, his mantle fell, Elisha picked it up and, saddened, went back to Jericho. The community of prophets in this city could contemplate everything from the other side of the river, where they had gathered to say farewell to Elijah. When they saw Elisha wielding the mantle and striking the water, as Elijah had just done before, and that the Jordan was divided leaving a dry path, they happily understood that the spirit of Elijah had rested on his disciple.

Elisha walked from one end of the kingdom of Israel to the other, promoting faith and God's commandments among the people. Kings consulted him about the dangers of war. Sometimes he had to confront them.

He worked many miracles.

The king of Syria sent Naaman, one of his army's generals, to the king of Israel with a letter of introduction, asking him to cure Naaman of his leprosy.

—Am I God? —said the king of Israel, tearing his garments. He feared the Syrians were setting him a trap.

Naaman had leprosy, and an Israelite servant girl of his wife told him that if he went to the prophet of Samaria, he would cure him for sure.

Elisha found out that the king had torn his

garments; so, he sent a message asking the king to send the leper to him. Naaman went to Elisha's house in his carriage. And his retinue of servants on horseback. Elisha came out of his house; and through his servant told him to go down to the Jordan and wash seven times and he would be clean. Naaman got angry; he expected more courtesy from the prophet, and things more difficult to do.

—Are the waters of Syria not better? —he said. And he gave orders to go back to Damascus. His servants said to him:

—If the prophet had told you to do something extraordinary, would you not have done it? All the more, you can do such an easy thing!

Naaman went to the Jordan and was clean. Elisha did not accept any of his presents.

(II Kings 2-8)

Jonah

GOD spoke to Jonah: «Set out for the great city of Niniveh and preach in it, for its sins are many». But the prophet, in order to flee from God's command, went down to Joppa, found a ship going to Tarshish (south of Spain), paid the fare and went aboard. A furious tempest arose, so that the sailors became frightened and threw the cargo into the sea in order to lighten the ship and avoid shipwreck. Each one cried to his god. Meanwhile, Jonah had gone down into the hold of the ship and lay there fast asleep. The captain found him and ordered him to rise up and call upon his God.

They feared that the storm was a punishment

of the gods, so they cast lots among them to find out who the culprit was. They singled out Jonah, who told them everything, and asked them to throw him into the sea. And immediately it was calm. God sent a large fish that swallowed Jonah. He remained in the belly of the fish three days and three nights, until it spewed him upon the shore. Once again God gave him the same order, and Jonah set out for Niniveh. It took three days to go through the city. Jonah entered the city and began to proclaim: «Forty days more and Niniveh shall be destroyed».

The Ninivites believed in Jonah and they repented for their sins. When the king of Niniveh found out, he came down from his throne, laid aside his robe and covered himself with sackcloth and ashes. He proclaimed a decree urging all the inhabitants to claim loudly to God, to fast and repent of their evil ways and injustices:

«Who knows, God may repent, so that we shall not perish?»

When God saw how they turned from their evil ways, He pitied them and did not carry out their destruction.

(Jonah)

119

Judith

HOLOFERNES was an Assyrian general; his powerful army advanced without any resistance; all the nations surrendered to him. Only Israel decided to organize strong resistance: Jerusalem and its temple shouldn't be profaned.

Judith was a God-fearing childless widow. She learned about the siege of the city, and asked to be allowed to come out of Bethulia with her maid; she wanted to do something in favour of Israel. At daybreak, she and her maid reached the enemy's encampment. The guard took her to Holofernes; she presented herself as a deserter.

A few days later, Judith accepted Holofernes' invitation to dine with him and his officers. One after the other they left the banquet hall, stumbling due to so much drinking. Holofernes fell on his bed befuddled by drunkeness, and Judith, with the general's own sword, beheaded him. She put the head in a leather purse, and pretending she was taking a walk with her maid, she headed towards Bethulia.

The gates were opened. When they heard Judith's words and saw Holofernes' head, the inhabitants of Bethulia came out with their weapons and horns. When the Syrian officers went to inform Holofernes of the imminent attack, they found him beheaded. They fled very fast and in great confusion.

All the people blessed Judith with these words: «You are the glory of Jerusalem, the surpassing joy of Israel; you are the splendid pride of our people».

(Judith)

Isaiah

THIS prophet, son of Amoz, had a vision: The Lord was sitting on his throne; a choir of seraphims were standing and singing: «Holy, Holy, Holy is the Lord of Hosts; all the earth is filled with his glory». One of them flew to him holding an ember

and touched his lips. He heard the voice of God who said: «Whom shall I send?». Then Isaiah answered: «Here I am, send me».

And God said to him: «Go and speak to this people».

And this is how Isaiah began his prophetic mission. He started it in the days of Jothan, Ahaz and Hezekah,

kings of Judah (742-677 B. C.).
King Ahaz, fearful of the coalition
between the kings of Syria and Israel, was
advised by Isaiah that his kingdom wouldn't
be conquered. In this meeting the prophet predicted among many other things, that the king of Assyria
would be the one to destroy Israel, and that day would come
when the Virgin would conceive and give birth to Immanuel
(God with us).

Shortly afterwards, Isaiah witnessed the destruction and
deportation of the inhabitants of Israel by the Assyrians.

In the fourteenth year of king Hezekiah, son of Ahaz,
king Sennacherib of Assyria conquered the strongholds of
Judah, and sent a general to the gates of Jerusalem to nego-
tiate its surrender. Hezekiah, trusting Isaiah, didn't yield, and
that very same night, thousands of Assyrian soldiers died of
a strange and contagious disease. Sennacherib went back to
Niniveh where he was assassinated by two of his sons.

Prophet Isaiah scourged idolatry and all kinds of sins
committed both by the people and by their kings.

(Isaiah)

Jeremiah

JEREMIAH, son of the priest Hilkiah, was brought up in the fear of God and according to the precepts of the law. He heard the word of God who said to him: «Before I formed you in the womb of your mother I knew you, and dedicated you as my messenger to the nations». Jeremiah objected to God's decision, saying he was too young and that he didn't know how to speak. The Lord touched his mouth and said: «Wherever I send you, you shall go; whatever I command you, you shall speak; I shall place my words in your mouth».

And Jeremiah began to deliver God's messages to the people at the gates of the temple and in the squares of Jerusalem. This happened during the troubled years of Josiah, Jehoiakim and Zedekiah, the last kings of Judah (627-587 B. C.).

Forcefully he denounced the sins of the people and their rulers: the apostasy, the injustice, the hardness of heart towards the poor, and the adulteries. He invited people to repent and convert, for God is more pleased by a faithful and just heart than by the stones, gold and sacrifices in the temple. Jeremiah sometimes complained to the Lord about the people not paying attention to him; but as soon as he was comforted by the Lord, he would go back to his preaching with new messages. He also announced the imminent fall of Jerusalem, destruction of the temple, and that all its treasure would be taken away to Babylon as booty of war.

Among those who listened to the prophet, some made fun of him, others were furious with him. Sometimes he was hit and scorned; one time he was jailed and another time he was thrown into a deep cess-pool up to his knees.

He had to endure the hard months of siege and destruction of Jerusalem and its temple by Nebuchadnezzar's army. In the conquest of the city he was protected by the king of Babylon's chief guard, who gave him freedom to go wherever he wished. Jeremiah decided to stay in Palestine with all the poor who were scattered all over the countryside of Judah. Sometime later he was captured by some rebels and taken to Egypt, where he died.

(Jeremiah)

Destruction of Jerusalem and exile

PHARAOH Neco II, king of Egypt, went up to wage war against Assyria. He asked king Josiah for permission to go across Judah. Josiah not only denied him passage, but confronted him in battle. Josiah died in the fight, and the pharaoh imposed Jehoiachim as the new king of Judah, with the obligation of paying him high taxes. Jehoiachim paid them taking silver and gold from the people. It was during

this hard servitude when Nebuchadnezzar, king of Babylon, subjugated Judah, and deported some Jews, among them the young Daniel.

Some years later, when Zedekia was the king, imposed by Nebuchadnezzar, Jerusalem rebelled against him. But Jerusalem was conquered once again; the walls, the temple and the royal palace were demolished, and the whole city was set on fire. All its inhabitants were deported to Babylon; only the very poor were left in the countryside of Judah to cultivate the vineyards.

(II Kings 23-25)

127

Ezekiel

EZEKIEL, son of the noble Ruzi, was deported to Babylon, together with king Jehoiachim (598 B. C.). This happened during the first siege of Jerusalem by Nebuchadnezzar.

He was living peacefully with the rest of the Jews who had settled in the land of the Chaldeans, always thinking of returning to his country soon. One day, while he was by the river Chebar, he was called by God, by means of a resplendent and mysterious vision, to be a prophet (593 B. C.).

God's main message given through Ezekiel, was to denounce the vices, both of those who lived in exile, and of those who still lived in Jerusalem. The sins he forcefully most often condemned were idolatry, adultery, perjury, murder and oppression of the poor. He foretold that his warnings would be fulfilled without fail. Also, that their obsession with sin was such, that there was no room for repentance, and for that reason God had left them at the mercy of their enemies.

Visions, parables and symbols are the means by which God communicated his messages to Ezekiel.

One day God ordered him to gather his belongings in front of everyone in the colony, as if he was going to emigrate; to breach the wall and, carrying his luggage, get out of the city through the open hole. In the morning God spoke to him: «Son of man, did not anyone of that rebellious house ask you what you were doing? Tell them...». With this symbolic action, God wanted to announce to them that king Zedekiah of Jerusalem would flee the city the same way, leaving it to its destruction (a few years later everything happened as foretold).

The destruction of the Holy city and its temple, and the definitive deportation to Babylon, was cause of reflection for many. Ezekiel urged them to repent; he reminded them that God is the shepherd of Israel and they the sheep of his flock. He gave them hope foretelling that the day would come when they could return to their land and become the seed of the future restoration of the People of God.

(Ezekiel)

Daniel

WHEN king Nebuchadnezzar sent the first expedition of his army to Judah (606 B. C.), he ordered that four youngsters of the nobility of Jerusalem be brought to Babylon and be instructed in all kinds of wisdom, and be taught the Chaldean language. Their training would take three years and then, if they were considered fit, they would be appointed to the service of Nebuchadnezzar. God granted the four boys intelligence and wisdom on every kind of subjects. Daniel was also gifted with an extraordinary power to interpret visions.

Nebuchadnezzar had a dream which worried him so much he couldn't sleep. He summoned his wise men and seers to interpret his dream. They admitted they were unable to do it, and the king ordered their death. This order also concerned Daniel. He prayed to the Lord, and God revealed to him the king's enigma. In order to save his own life and that of his companions he came up to the king and explained his dream: There was a huge statue; its head was made out of gold; its torso and arms of silver; its abdomen and loins of bronze; its thighs of iron, and its feet of clay and iron. When he was contemplating it, a stone fell down from a mountain, without a human hand being put to it, and struck the feet of the statue which fell apart crumbling into dust. But the stone became a great mountain and filled the whole Earth.

«This was the dream», said Daniel; and this is the interpretation: «You, o king, are the head of gold; a kingdom of silver will take your place; another one of bronze will follow; later on there shall be another kingdom strong as iron, which will be weaker as it mixes with fragile clay. The stone which fell from the mountain without human intervention, is the new kingdom God will create and it will endure for ever by means of this dream, God has revealed to the king what shall be in the future».

Nebuchadnezzar fell down and confessed before Daniel: «Your God is God of gods and Lord of kings». He gave Daniel generous presents; he made him ruler of the whole province of Babylon and chief over all wise men.

(Daniel)

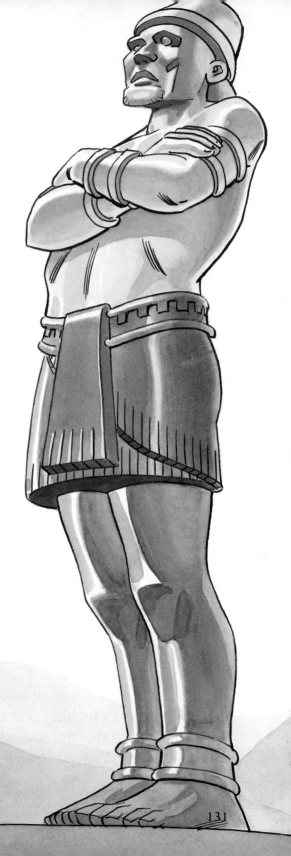

131

Esther

MORDECAI was one of the Jews deported in Nebuchadnezzar's time. He had adopted as a daughter an orphan niece of his, named Esther. Among the maidens introduced to Ahasuerus, Esther was the chosen one to be the queen.

In those days, Haman was appointed the second one in command after the king. Everyone, except Mordecai, prostrated before him when he came into the royal palace; for this reason Haman was furious against him. When he found out that Mordecai belonged to the Jewish race, he decreed that all the Jews be executed.

When Mordecai heard about it, he tore his garments as a sign of sorrow and sadness, he put on sackcloth and covered his head with ashes. Then he sent Haman's decree to Esther, begging her to invoke the Lord and speak to the king in behalf of their people.

Esther spent three days in prayer and fasting; then, dressed in her best clothes, went to Ahasuerus to invite him to a banquet she had prepared for the king and Haman. During the banquet, Ahasuerus, to show his satisfaction, said to Esther that she could ask for anything she wanted, and he would grant it at once, whatever it might be.

Esther spoke up and begged for her own life, since she was also a Jew, and for the life of her people, for all of them were doomed to death by Haman's orders. When Ahasuerus heard the story, he leaped up in anger and, furious, sentenced Haman to death. He was executed in the same gallows he had prepared for Mordecai.

Immediately messengers were dispatched to all the provinces to inform about the annulment of Haman's decree. The Jews were given back all the favors they had enjoyed before. Thus, their anguish and terror changed into jubilation and happiness. All this happened thanks to Esther's mediation in favor of her people.

(Esther 1; 5; 10)

Tobit

TOBIT, like so many other Israelites, was deported to Niniveh, together with his wife Anna. From his youth he always loved and served the Lord, and lived in his presence all the time.

It happened that one time, droppings from a nest fell into his eyes and went blind.

Tobit had a son, named Tobiah, and told him to look for a man acquainted with the roads who would travel with him to collect some money. Tobiah met a young man ready to guide him.

Tobit gave them the receipts, and they set out on their journey; a dog followed them. They made camp by the Tigris river. Tobiah went down to wash his feet and suddenly a fish threatened him with its mouth wide open. He shouted. The young companion told him to take the fish out of the water.

—Take out its heart, liver and gall and keep them with you, for they make useful medicine —said the young man.

They travelled for several more days. The guide proposed that they should spend the night at Raquel's, a kinsman of Tobit, he advised Tobiah to ask for his daughter Sarah in marriage, saying that God had kept her for him.

While the wedding feast was in progress, the young man took the receipts and went to the city; then, he collected the ten talents of silver.

Finally, they began their return journey to Niniveh. Tobiah, following his guide's advise, put the fish's gall on his father's eyes, and he miraculously regained sight. The whole house was filled with joy. Tobit could see again; his son had returned home with a beautiful wife, and they had enough money to live on. God had been very generous with them. When Tobit spoke to the young man to give him as his salary half of what they had brought, he said to them:

—I am Raphael, one of the seven angels who bring up the prayers of the saints before God.

Then he disappeared.

(Tobit)

Job

THERE was a man in the land of Uz named Job. He was a blameless and upright man, who feared God and avoided evil.

One day God asked Satan if he had noticed his faithful servant Job. The Devil replied that if Job did not rebel, it was because everything around him was in his favour; but if his wealth and property were affected, surely he would blaspheme like everybody else. Then God gave Satan permission to do whatever he wished, but only not to lay a hand upon his person. And it happened that in only one day all misfortunes came upon Job: his oxen, camels and asses were stolen; his servants were murdered and his sons and daughters died crushed under the rubble of the house where they were eating together. Job cast himself prostrate upon the ground, and said: «God gave and God has taken away; blessed be his name».

God was pleased by Job's attitude, and again, Satan questioned the fidelity of God's servant. The Devil said: «All that a man has will he give for his life, but if his health is affected he will blaspheme». And God said: «He is in your power; only spare his life». Then Job was stricken with severe ulcers from the soles of his feet to the crown of his head. His wife urged him to curse God. But Job said:

—You speak like a senseless woman. If we accept good things from God, should we not accept evil?

Job said over and over that he had not done evil. He wondered: Why does evil exist?

God intervened asking Job many questions he couldn't answer. Finally God said: «Suffering is hard to understand; I can measure it, and I dispense it as it pleases me. Trust me!»

And Job's health was restored; he had more children and doubled his riches, and he became even more generous with the needy than before.

(Job)

The return from exile

THE Jews had spent about sixty years living in exile. Cyrus, the founder of the Persian empire, defeated the Assyrians, and Babylon fell into his power. In the first year (538 B. C.) he issued a proclamation encouraging the Jews to return to his country and rebuild the temple; he urged those

who would stay to cooperate with gold, silver and other donations for the house of God in Jerusalem; he gave back 5.400 sacred vases which had been stolen by the Babylonians.

With religious fervour 42.360 people set out, under the leadership both of Zerubbabel, appointed governor of Judah, and Joshua, High Priest. Some settled in Jerusalem, and others in their own cities. During the first months they kept themselves busy restoring their houses and fields. On the seventh month all gathered in Jerusalem. Jeshua and Zerubbabel built up and altar and offered sacrifices to God. A big celebration took place. Everyone made donations for the stonecutters to start cutting stones, and the carpenters to work on the cedar wood, which they imported from Lebanon.

In the second year, they started to lay out the foundation of the temple, which was finished in the sixth year of Darius (516 B. C.), a great celebration took place on that occasion.

(Ezra 1-7)

140

ZRA was a scribe, a faithful Jew in his fulfillment of the Law of Moses; he was devoted to teaching it to the Jewish people who had remained in exile. King Artaxerxes of Persia allowed him to go to Palestine with the faithful Jews, to teach and promote the fulfillment of the Law of God.

Ezra and his devoted group of followers arrived in Jerusalem in the seventh year of Artaxerxes' reign (458 B. C.). Very soon he found out why the Jews had abandoned their fidelity to God. He summoned assemblies, he read and explained the Law of Moses. The Jews recognized their deviations, they did penance and renewed their covenant with God.

Ezra always felt protected by Nehemiah, since the latter arrived in Jerusalem thirteen years afterwards.

NOTE: The synagogue, as a meeting place and center of upbringing in the religious life, has its origin in the exile of Babylon. At Saturday and holy day Jewish meetings they offered prayers and sang psalms; they read the scrolls containing the Law of Moses, and explained it to the people. Ezra was the organizer of this kind of religious services, and he took them to Palestine. This is how he laid down the foundation of the religiosity and love for the Law which would last with the Jewish people in Palestine until the advent of the Messiah.

(Ezra and Nehemiah)

Nehemiah

WHEN Nehemiah was king Artaxerxes' chief cupbearer, he learned that Jerusalem was an open city, because its walls continued in ruins. He asked for permission to go and rebuild them. Artaxerxes gave him letters in order to facilitate his work. As soon as he arrived in Jerusalem, he inspected the walls for three nights, and prepared the project.

He summoned the city authorities and explained to them the reason for his coming to Jerusalem. They became enthusiastic about the project; the walls were divided into sections and each one of them was assigned to groups of families.

Some influential people of Samaria were upset about Jerusalem being fortified and tried by all means to stop the work. Nehemiah found out they were plotting to kill the builders and also himself. For many days they didn't take off their clothes, not even to sleep, neither did they put aside their weapons. Working and watching, they finished the work. Jerusalem was again a walled city.

Nehemiah returned to Artaxerxes' service; but once in a while he went back to Jerusalem to give support to the religious reformation God had entrusted to Ezra.

NOTE: Even though, since the deportation to Babylon, Palestine was always subjected to different empires, its religion and Law were respected and protected throughout the centuries. Until...

(Ezra and Nehemiah)

The Maccabees

ANTIOCHUS IV Epiphanes conquered Egypt. On his return, he went through Jerusalem and the whole of Palestine (169 B. C.). He ransacked the temple treasures; he killed many Jews and returned to his land, north of Palestine. Two years later he sent a tax collector, with a large escort, to all the cities in Judea. In Jerusalem many of its inhabitants were murdered; the city was ransacked and set on fire.

On top of this, Antiochus published a decree, and by it, all the nations under his power had to give up their own laws and religion to become a unified nation.

Many Jews remained faithful to God's covenant. Like that mother and her seven sons. One by one, from the oldest to the youngest one, and in the pre-

sence of the others and also
of their mother, were mutila-
ted, tortured in many ways, and burnt. During the torture,
their own mother gave them courage. That persecution was a
cruel one in the whole of Palestine.

Some Jews hid themselves in the caves in the desert. The
king's patrols found them on a Saturday and, in order not to
break it fighting, around thousand people let themselves be
executed without resistance.

(I and II Maccabees)

Mattathias

THE priest Matthathias lived in Modein. He had five sons: John, Simon, Judas, Eleazar and Jonathan. Envoys of king Antiochus arrived in Modein to force apostasy and the offering of sacrifices to the idols. Mattathias refused saying:

—Although everyone obeys the king, my sons and myself will follow the Law of our God.

He still was speaking when a Jew went up to offer a sacrifice to the idols. Mattathias, burning by his zeal for the honor of God couldn't

restrain himself and killed him on the altar. At the same time he turned towards the king's envoy and killed him too; he tore down the altar and shouted:

—Let everyone who is keeping the Covenant follow after me! Thereupon he fled to the mountains with his sons.

Courageous men, faithful to the Law, kept joining him, for they couldn't stand Antiochus' ignominies.

Shortly before he died Mattathias summoned his followers and said to them: «Do not attack on the sabbath; but if someone attacks you, you will fight though it might be the day of rest; do not act like those brothers of ours in the desert who let themselves be killed for keeping the sabbath. Be strong and fight for our God and his Law». Then he appointed captain the bravest of his sons, Judas, nicknamed Maccabeus (166 B. C.).

(I and II Maccabees)

New Testament

The Messiah

We have read throughout the Old Testament how God reveals himself to a people, chosen to be instrumental for this revelation to reach all mankind. At the same time we have seen the adventures of these people, always struggling between fidelity to God and departure from Him, the latter always as a consequence of their sins.

For sin is the worst and the only real evil for the man who commits it, because it is a free act of rebellion against God.

Sin is man's permanent enemy.

To put a stop to sin means to save man. And God had planned salvation from the very beginning.

The savior will be a member of the human race.

The prophets, though with a distant and imperfect vision, foretold that the savior would be a descendant of David; that a virgin would conceive the Emmanuel, «God with us»; that he would be born in Bethlehem; that he would suffer for the sins of men; that he would establish an everlasting kingdom of grace, of holiness, of forgiveness for all mankind; that he would come within a period of seventy weeks of years...

The Jewish people lived in the expectancy of his arrival.

In the year 63 B. C. Pompeius, a Roman general conquered Palestine. This event marks the immediate background in the life of the promised and expected Messiah: Jesus, true God and true man, who will seal the New Testament with his blood.

The books of the New Testament are: the four Gospels (according St. Matthew, St. Mark, St. Luke and St. John), the Acts of the Apostles, the Letters of St. Paul, St. John, St. James, St. Jude and the Revelation.

The Annunciation

NAZARETH was a little town in the region of Galilee, north of Palestine, by the slopes of a hill. It had a well where the town girls filled their jugs. On top of the hill there was a synagogue to hold religious services on the Sabbath. Its streets were irregular, with slopes and ditches.

A certain girl lived in that town. She was betrothed to a man named Joseph; however, she had made the vow to remain a virgin. The virgin's name was Mary.

One day the angel Gabriel, sent from God, came down to the house where she lived, and said to her:

—Rejoice, full of grace. The Lord is with you. Blessed are you among women.

Mary was deeply troubled by his words and wondered what such an extraordinary greeting meant. Then, the angel said:

—Do not fear, Mary, you have found favour with God. You shall conceive and bear a son, and give him the name of Jesus (God saves). Great will be his dignity and He will be called Son of the Most High. The Lord God will give him the throne of David, his father. He will rule over the house of Jacob for ever, and his reign will be without end.

Mary said to the angel:

—How can this be since I do not know man?

The angel answered her:

—The Holy Spirit will come upon you, and the power of the Most High will overshadow you; hence, the holy offspring to be born will be called Son of God. Know that Elizabeth your kinswoman has conceived a son in her old age; she who was thought to be sterile is now in her sixth month, for nothing is impossible with God.

And Mary said:

—I am the servant of the Lord. Let it be done to me as you say.

With that the angel left her, and in that instant the Son of God was made man in the womb of Mary. This event took place on the year 748 of the foundation of Rome.

(Lk. 1, 26-38)

The Visitation

FILLED with humble joy Mary called to mind the angel's words, and realized that her kinswoman Elizabeth might need her help.

Thereapon Mary set out, proceeding in haste into the hill country to a town of Judah. While on her way she thought of the Great Secret she was carrying in her womb.

She entered Zacharian's house and greeted Elizabeth. When Elizabeth heard Mary's greeting, the baby in her womb leapt with glee. She was filled with the Holy Spirit and cried out in a loud voice:

—Blessed are you among women and blessed is the fruit of your womb. But who am I that the mother of my Lord should come to me? Blessed are you who have trusted, for everything the Lord has said will be fulfilled.

Then Mary said:

—My soul proclaims the greatness of the Lord, my saviour, for he has looked upon his servant in her lowliness. All ages to come shall call me blessed. For God who is mighty has done great things for me. Holy is his name; his mercy is from age to age on those who fear him. He has shown might with his arm; he has concussed the proud, he has deposed the mighty; he has raised the lowly; the hungry he has given every good thing, while the rich he has sent empty away. He has upheld Israel his servant, ever mindful of his mercy.

Mary remained with Elizabeth about three months, and then returned to Nazareth.

(Lk. 1, 39-56)

155

Joseph, Mary's husband

JOSEH was a craftsman. For this reason he was well known in Nazareth. Who, in a small town doesn't need the services of a craftsman once in awhile?

Joseph was betrothed to Mary. By such a commitment they were obliged to fidelity; however, they didn't live

together yet. It was during this period of time that Mary conceived miraculously by the Holy Spirit.

Joseph trusted his wife's honesty, nevertheless, he was confused; but being an upright man he was unwilling to expose her. Then, an angel of the Lord appeared and said to him:

—Joseph, son of David, have no fear about taking Mary as your wife. It is by the Holy Spirit that she has conceived this child. She is to have a son and you are to name him Jesus because he will save his people from their sins.

Joseph was filled with joy, and spoke to her. From then on he accepted his privilege of being the chaste spouse of Mary and the foster father of Jesus.

God has bestowed upon him all the human and supernatural gifts in accordance with his extraordinary mission.

(Mt. 1, 18-25)

Birth of Jesus

CAESAR Augustus published a decree ordering a census, and Joseph had to walk the great distance between Nazareth and Bethlehem to register with Mary, his wife.

When they arrived they didn't find room at the inn and they had to take refuge in a cave near the town, which was used to shelter sheep. While they were there the days of her confinement were completed and she gave birth to Jesus. She wrapped him in swaddling clothes and laid him in a manger.

Some shepherds that night saw a shining angel who proclaimed the good news:

—You have nothing to fear. I come to bring you good news of

great joy. The Saviour, who is the Messiah, the Lord has been born today in Bethlehem. You will recognize him because he is wrapped in swaddling clothes, lying in a humble stable.

A host of the heavenly army joined the angel and exclaimed loudly:

—Glory be to God on high and peace to men who love the Lord!

The shepherds hurried near and found Mary, Joseph and the Child, lying in the stable, and worshiped Him.

(Lk. 2, 1-20)

𝕻resentation in the temple

O N the eighth day of his birth, Joseph brought the child to the temple for his circumcision, and gave him the name of Jesus, as the angel had said.

There lived in Jerusalem at the time an elderly man, just and God-fearing, named Simeon. Like all the pious Jews he awaited and prayed for the advent of the Messiah.

After forty days from the Child's birth, they went up to Jerusalem to visit the temple for Mary's purification and the presentation of the Child to the Lord.

Simeon, inspired by the Holy Spirit, came to the temple, and met Joseph and Mary carrying the Child in her arms.

The old man asked them to let him take the Child, and Mary placed him into his arms. Then Simeon, looking at him said:

—Now, Lord, you can dismiss your servant in peace; for my eyes have witnessed the salvation of all the peoples and the glory of Israel.

Then with sadness, he said to Mary:

—And for yourself, a sword shall pierce your soul.

There was also a certain prophetess, Anna by name; she was eighty-four years old, a widow who served the Lord in fasting and prayer. She recognized the Child and talked with enthusiasm, about the Child, to all who looked forward to the deliverance of Israel.

(Lk. 2, 21-39)

161

The Wise Men

HEROD was the king of Palestine; he became greatly disturbed when Wise Men from the East arrived in Jerusalem inquiring about the new king of the Jews; they had seen his star at its rising and had come to worship him. Herod summoned his scribes and chief priests. They told him that, according to the prophecies the Christ was to be born in Bethlehem. Then Herod, after finding out the exact time of the star's appearance, sent them to Bethlehem. He asked them, when they found the Child to inform him, so he would go and adore him too.

By then Joseph and Mary had left the cave. With great joy for the Wise Men, the star reappeared ahead of them until it came to a standstill in Bethlehem over the place where the Child was. They adored him and presented him with gifts of gold, frankincense and myrrh.

That night the angel of the Lord told the Wise Men to return to their country without seeing Herod. He also told Joseph to flee to Egypt, for Herod was going to search for the Child to kill him, and stay there until he advised him to return.

Herod became furious because the Wise Men had deceived him; then he ordered the massacre of all the boys in Bethlehem who were two years old or under. Most likely this was the last of his many crimes, since he died in the spring of the year 750 of the foundation of Rome.

Archelaus, as blood thirsty as his father, began to reign in Judea, where Bethlehem was located; Herod Antipas, the other son, more gentle, inherited Galilee. That's why, Joseph, when the angel told him that

there wasn't any danger for the
Child, went to live in Nazareth
instead of Bethlehem.

Their exile in Egypt had lasted
some two years.

(Mt. 2, 1-23)

Jesus in the midst of the Teachers

THE Child grew in size and strength in Nazareth. From running about the house, he went out into the streets; he began to discover the world with his human eyes, and played with his peers. He was filled with the grace of God and with human graces. He performed all the errands he was asked by Joseph and Mary, and went to the sinagogue to learn the Law of Moses.

His parents used to go every year to Jerusalem for the feasts of Passover. When Jesus turned twelve, the age for a good Israelite to fulfill the precepts of the Law, the three of them went up to Jerusalem. Caravans departed from every town.

At the end of the feasts, caravans were organized for their return by groups of men and groups of women going the same way, and children always running about between the two groups.

After the first day's journey Jesus didn't show up. Joseph and Mary looked for him amongst the youngsters and adults, but no one had seen him throughout the journey; heartbroken they returned to Jerusalem. They searched for him in anguish, until they went to the temple. Mary and Joseph looked on and saw him in the midst of the teachers who were listening and asking him questions. All were amazed at his intelligence and answers. Mary got closer and with affection said to him:

—Son, why have you done this to us? Your father and I have been searching for you in sorrow.

—Why did you search for me? Did you not know I had to be in my father's house?

Jesus grew up from adolescence to become a young man. He learned from Joseph to be an artisan and, when he died, Jesus took over the workshop until he was thirty years old.

(Lk. 2, 40-52)

John the Baptist

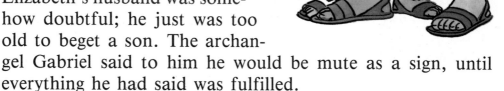

THE child conceived by Elizabeth, Mary's kinswoman, was called John. The angel that appeared to Zechariah to announce this miraculous conception, told him that such had to be his name. And furthermore, the angel said, he would go before the Lord to prepare for Him a perfect people.

Zechariah had the vision of the angel when he was fulfilling his functions as a priest in the temple, when it was his turn. Elizabeth's husband was somehow doubtful; he just was too old to beget a son. The archangel Gabriel said to him he would be mute as a sign, until everything he had said was fulfilled.

When John was born, Zechariah was able to speak and proclaimed:

—Blessed be the Lord God... for He has given a mighty Saviour to the house of David, fulfilling what the prophets promised. —And he added, looking at his son—: And you, o Child, shall be called prophet of the Most High, for you will give to his people a knowledge of salvation through forgiveness of their sins.

When John grew up he lived in the desert to mature in spirit until the day he made his public appearance.

Then he began to preach about the whole region of the Jordan. He was clothed in a garment of camel's hair, tied with a leather belt. He ate grasshoppers and wild honey. He forcefully encouraged people to repent for their sins, and proclaimed that the kingdom of God was near. The whole of Palestine was moved by his words, and many came forward to be baptized in the waters of the Jordan.

Herod Antipas had put him in chains because of Herodias, his brother's wife, who was living with the king. John openly reprehended this kind of behaviour. The king organized a banquet for his courtiers; Herodia's daughter danced for the guests. Herod liked it so much that he swore to give her anything she asked for. The girl consulted with her mother who advised her to ask for John the Baptist's head, to be presented on a platter. Herod satisfied her wish by beheading him.

His disciples carried his body away and buried it.

(Lk. 1, 5-25; 3, 1-6; Mt. 14, 3-12)

167

Baptism of Jesus

THE Gospels, when they narrate the public life of John and Jesus, place it within the framework of contemporary history: «In the fifteenth year of the rule of Tiberius Caesar (779 of Rome), when Pontius Pilate was procurator of Judea, and Herod tetrarch of

Galilee; the word of God was spoken to John in the desert».

John performed his mission in the Jordan, and from there he touched the people of Israel, to such an extent that many were wondering whether he might be the Messiah. John answered them all by saying: «I am not the Messiah; I am baptizing you in water, only as a penance; but there is one to come, of whom I am not fit to loosen his sandal strap, who will baptize you in the Holy Spirit and in fire».

One day Jesus, coming from Nazareth, appeared before John at the Jordan to be baptized by him. But John knew by inner revelation who he was, and refused saying:

—I should be baptized by you, yet you come to me.

—Give in for now. We must fulfill all justice.

So John gave in and let Jesus be baptized. As soon as Jesus came out of the water, being in prayer, the sky opened and the Spirit of God descended as a dove and hovered over Him. With that a voice from the heavens said:

—This is my beloved Son, my favour rests on Him.

(Lk. 3, 1-23; Mt. 3, 13-17)

Jesus is tempted in the desert

JESUS, after being baptized, left the Jordan and was led into the desert by the Spirit. Jesus spent forty days in prayer and fasting. During this period of time he had to endure the devil's temptations on three occasions. Due to his long fasting, Jesus was hungry; so Satan approached and said to him:

—If you are the Son of God command these stones to turn into bread, and eat.

—Not by bread alone does man live, but by every word that comes from the mouth of God —Jesus answered.

Then the devil took Jesus and set him into the pinnacle of the temple, and said to him:

—If you are the Son of God, throw yourself down; nothing

will happen to you because the angels will support you with their hands, according to the scripture.

—Scripture also has it: «You shall not put the Lord to the test» —Jesus answered.

Finally the devil took him up to a very high mountain and displayed before him the magnificence and the glory of the kingdoms of the world.

—I will give you all these riches and the honor of being the ruler of all these kingdoms if you worship me.

Then Jesus answered him:

—Away with you, Satan! Scripture has it: «The Lord your God you shall adore and him only shall you serve».

At that the devil left him and the angels waited on him in love.

(Mt. 4, 1-11; Lk. 4, 1-13)

171

The first Disciples

WHEN Jesus finished his forty days of solitude in the desert, he went back to the valley of the Jordan. John the Baptist was there with two of his disciples, Andrew and the very young John. The Baptist saw Jesus coming towards him and exclaimed:

—Look! There is the Lamb of God who takes away the sin of the world. I don't know Him, but I have seen that This is truly the Son of God.

When the two disciples heard this, they followed Jesus. Then Jesus noticed them following Him, and asked them:

—What are you looking for?

—Rabbi, where do you stay?

—Come and see.

They stayed with him all that day. Andrew talked about

Jesus to his brother Simon, and brought him to meet Jesus. Jesus looked at him and said:

—You are Simon, son of John; your name shall be Cephes (which means Rock = Peter).

On their way back to Galilee, Jesus came upon Philip and said to him: «Follow me». Philip as well as Andrew, John and Peter, were from Bethsaida, a fishing village by the lake of Tiberias. Then Philip met Nathanael, from Cana, and told him that Jesus, from Nazareth, was the Messiah.

—Can anything good come from Nazareth? —he asked.

—Come and see for yourself! —Philip replied.

When Jesus saw Nathanael coming toward him, he said:

—Behold a true Israelite in whom there is no guile.

—How do you know me?

—Before Philip called you, I saw you under the fig tree.

—Rabbi, you are the Son of God. —Said Nathanael, amazed by what Jesus just had said.

(Jn. 1, 29-51)

The wedding at Cana

MORE disciples joined Jesus on his way from the Jordan to Nazareth. At Nathanael's town there was a wedding. Jesus and his disciples had been invited. The mother of Jesus was likewise there.

At a certain point the wine ran out. The mother of Jesus came to tell him what had happened.

—Woman, how does this concern of yours involve me? My hour has not yet come.

Mary, nevertheless, instructed those waiting on table:

—Do whatever he tells you.

There were at hand six stone jars for the Jewish ceremonial washing when people entered to the house. Jesus ordered the waiters:

—Fill those jars with water.

When they were filled to the brim He said:

—Now, draw some out and take it to the waiter in charge.

The chief steward was surprised on account of the wine's quality, and called the groom over and remarked to him:

—People usually serve the choice wine first and at the end they serve a lesser vintage. You have done it the other way around.

Jesus performed the first of his signs at Cana in Galilee.

(Jn. 2, 1-11)

The vendors in the temple

THE Jewish Passover was celebrated at the beginning of spring. As the feast was near, Jesus went up to Jerusalem. In the temple precincts there were merchants with oxen, sheep and doves in cages; the money-changers also had their tables in the temple area. The great multitude of outsiders who came to Jerusalem were able to buy the animals needed for the sacrifices, or exchange Greek or Roman coins for Jewish currency. Because of the Passover, the merchants were doing good business in the temple precints.

Jesus made a kind of whip of cords and drove the vendors out of the temple; he knocked over the money-changers' tables, spilling their coins, and said:

—Stop turning my Father's house into a market-place!

After this havoc, the chiefs of the Jews came to Jesus and asked him:

—What sign can you show us to do these things?

—Destroy this temple and in three days I will raise it up.

—This temple took forty-six years to build, and you are going to raise it up in three days?

Actually Jesus was talking about the temple of his body.

(Jn. 2, 13-22; 3, 1-21)

177

Jesus by Jacob's well

JESUS spent some time in Judea. And then he decided to go back to Galilee where he heard that John the Baptist had been put in chains; also that the pharisees were suspicious of the many disciples who were joining him.

Jesus, going through Samaria, reached Jacob's well, near the town of Shechem. The hour was about noon and Jesus, tired from his journey, sat down at the well. In the meantime, his disciples went to town to buy something to eat. Then a woman came to draw water. For centuries Samaritans and Jews were enemies. Nevertheless Jesus asked her for a drink of water. She said:

—How come that you being a Jew ask me, a Samaritan woman, for a drink?

—If only you recognized who it is that is asking you for water, you would have asked him instead, and he would have given you living water... which will leap up to eternal life and quench thirst for ever.

—I can see you are a
prophet: explain to me if it is on this mountain or in Jerusalem where God must be worshipped.

—The hour has come when you will worship the father
neither in Jerusalem nor here. God is spirit, and those who
worship him must worship in spirit and truth.

—I know a Messiah is coming; he will tell us everything.

—I who speak to you am He.

The woman left her water jar and went off into the town
to tell the people all that Jesus had said to her.

(Jn. 4, 1-42)

179

The miraculous draught of fish

JESUS' prestige had extended everywhere. One time when he was walking by the lake, the crowd pressed in on him to hear his teachings. There were two boats moored by the lake. Their owners, Andrew and his brother Simon, were washing their nets. Jesus got into Simon's boat and asked him to pull out a short distance from the shore. From the boat he kept teaching the crowds who were listening to him from the shore. When he had finished speaking, he told Simon and Andrew to put out into deep water to fish. Simon said to him:

—Master, the whole night through we have toiled and have caught nothing; but if you say so I will lower the net.

Upon doing this they caught such a great number of fish that their net was at breaking point. They signaled to their mates in the other boat to come and help them. These mates were the young John and his brother James. The two boats were so full that they nearly sank.

At the sight of this, Simon fell at the feet of Jesus saying:

—Leave me, Lord, for I am a sinful man.

—From now on you will be catching men.

With that they arrived at the shore and Jesus asked Simon and Andrew to follow him. He did the same with James and John. They left everything and followed him.

(Lk. 5, 1-11)

A paralytic is forgiven

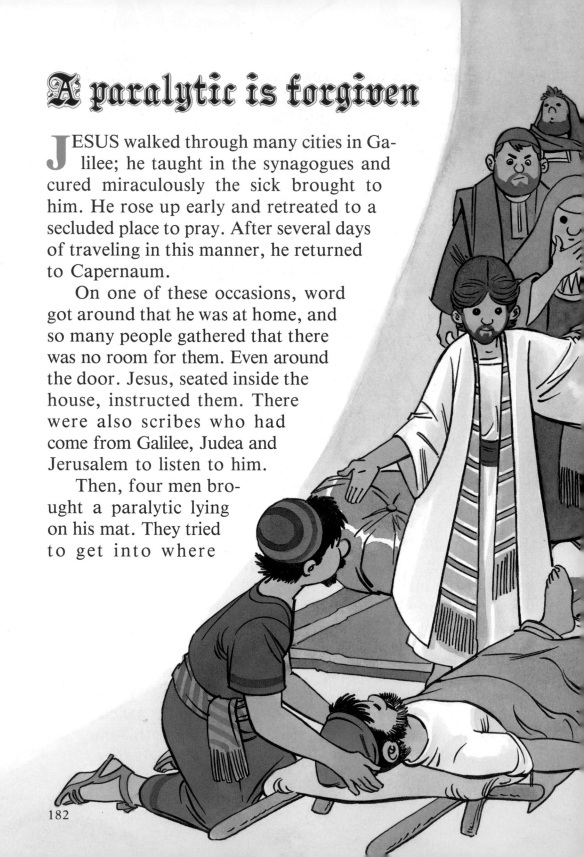

JESUS walked through many cities in Galilee; he taught in the synagogues and cured miraculously the sick brought to him. He rose up early and retreated to a secluded place to pray. After several days of traveling in this manner, he returned to Capernaum.

On one of these occasions, word got around that he was at home, and so many people gathered that there was no room for them. Even around the door. Jesus, seated inside the house, instructed them. There were also scribes who had come from Galilee, Judea and Jerusalem to listen to him.

Then, four men brought a paralytic lying on his mat. They tried to get into where

Jesus was; but they were unable to get through the crowd standing at the door. They climbed the outer stairs up to the terrace, and made a hole over the spot where Jesus was. Then, by means of ropes, they let down the mat on which the paralytic was lying. When Jesus saw the faith of those men, who were looking through the hole in the roof, he said to the paralytic:

—My son, your sins are forgiven.

The scribes, who were sitting inside, thought that Jesus was committing blasphemy, as he dared to say he forgave sins, because only God could forgive them.

Jesus, being aware of their thoughts, asked them:

—Which is easier, to say to the paralytic, "your sins are forgiven", or to say, "stand up, pick up your mat, and walk again"? That you may know that I have authority on earth to forgive sins...

—He said to the paralytic— I command you, stand up! Pick up your mat and go home!

The man was cured, and at once, stood up and left.

(Mk. 2, 1-12)

Choice of the Apostles

JESUS knew that his mission was to save all mankind. However, his visible presence upon earth was going to be very short. He had to choose some men who would continue his mission throught the centuries.

Jesus retreated to a secluded place and spent the whole night in prayer with his Heavenly Father. At daybreak he called his disciples and selected twelve of them to be his Apostles, live with him and, later, be sent to preach. He chose Simon, to whom he gave the name Peter; and Andrew, his brother; James and John, Zebedee's sons, to whom he gave the name of Sons of Thunder; Philip and Bartholomew; Matthew, who was called to follow him when he was sitting at his tax-collector's table; Judas Thaddaeus, James of Alphaeus' brother; and Judas Iscariot, the one who would betray him. On a certain occasion he gave them, among many others, these instructions:

—Provide yourselves with neither gold, nor silver, nor copper: the workman, after all, is worth his keep.

—If anyone does not receive you or listen to you, leave that town, and once outside it shake its dust from your feet, as a sign against them.

—See that I am sending you out like sheep among wolves. Be prudent.

—On my account you will be slandered and persecuted.

—Do not fear those who deprive the body of life but cannot destroy the soul.

—He who welcomes you welcomes me; he who despises you despises me.

Later on Jesus was bestowing upon them the powers they would need to carry on the Salvation of the world.

(Lk. 6, 12-16; Mt. 10, 5-42)

The Sermon on the Mount

AFTER calling his Apostles, Jesus was coming down with them, when he met a great crowd of people from Judea, Jerusalem and from the coasts of Tyre and Sidon. They had come to hear him and be cured of their illnesses. Jesus sat down and began to teach them the beatitudes:

—Blessed are the poor in spirit.

—Blessed are the sorrowing.

—Blessed are they who hunger and thirst for holiness.

—Blessed are the merciful.

—Blessed are the clean of heart.

—Blessed are the persecuted for their faith.

—You are the salt of the earth and the light of the world.

—Love your enemies and pray for those who persecute you.

—Do your good deeds only before the eyes of God.

—You cannot serve God and money.

—Forgive, and you shall be forgiven.

—Give, and it shall be given to you.

When Jesus finished teaching the crowds, they wondered about his doctrine and because he spoke to them with great authority.

(Mt. 5-7; Lk. 6, 17-49)

187

The widow's son

DURING his teaching throughout Galilee Jesus went to a town called Naim. His disciples and a large crowd accompanied him.

Then, a funeral procession passed by Jesus. A young man, the only son of a widowed mother, was going to be buried. The Lord was moved with pity, and said to her:

—Do not cry.

And stepping forward he made a sign to the pallbearers to stop and, touching the litter, he said:

—Young man, I say to you, get up!

The dead man sat up and began to speak. Then Jesus, taking him by his hand, gave him back to his mother.

Fear seized them all and they began to praise God, saying:

—A great prophet has risen among us. —And again—: God has visited his people.

The fame of this miracle spread throughout Judea and the surrounding country.

(Lk. 7, 11-17)

The storm on the lake

AS on other occasions, Jesus spoke to the people from a boat, not far from the shore.

At sunset, when he finished, he wanted to go across the lake to the land of the Gerasenes. He was tired, and fell asleep in the stern. While sailing, a bad squall blew up and the storm broke.

The disciples, though they were fishermen in that lake, could not overcome the waves, and full of fear, woke him up shouting:

—Lord, save us! We are lost!

Jesus said to them:

—Why are you so terrified, men of little faith?

Then he stood up on the boat and rebuked the sea:

—Quiet! Be still!

At that the wind fell off and everything grew calm. The disciples, amazed, kept saying to one another:

—Who can this be that even the wind and the sea obey him.

(Mt. 8, 23-27; Mk. 4, 35-40)

The daughter of Jairus

NOW when Jesus had crossed back to Capernaum in the boat, a large crowd was already waiting for him. One of the officials of the synagogue, named Jairus, begged Jesus to go to his house: his twelve year old daughter was dying.

Jesus went off together with Jairus; a large crowd followed, pushing against Jesus. A woman came up behind him and put her hand on his cloak. Jesus asked:

—Who has touched me?

—You can see the crowd pressing upon you and you ask, who touched me? —asked Simon Peter in amazement.

Jesus kept looking around.

The woman, realizing she had been discovered, but feeling

cured, fell at the feet of Jesus: she told him in front of the crowd, that she had been afflicted with haemorrhage for twelve years, and that she had spent all that she had on physicians, yet she got no relief.

—Be trustful; it is your faith that has cured you; go in peace —Jesus said to her.

He had not finished speaking when people came to notify Jairus that his daughter was dead. Jesus heard it and said:

—Do not be afraid; only have faith.

As they approached the house they heard the noise of people wailing and crying loudly. Then Jesus put them all out. He entered where the girl lay dead, took her hand and said:

—Little girl, I say to you, get up!

The girl stood up immediately and began to walk.

(Mk. 5, 21-43)

The miracle of the loaves and fishes

JESUS and his Apostles went off in a boat towards the territory of Bethsaida. To a deserted place to rest for a day: they were always so busy that they did not even have time to eat. People saw

them leaving, but they got to know where they were heading to, and followed them on foot round the lake.

It was now getting late and the Apostles advised Jesus to dismiss the people, so they could buy something to eat in the neighbouring towns. Jesus answered:

—You give them something to eat.

Andrew said that there was a boy who had five barley loaves and a couple of dry fish, and added:

—But what good is this for so many?

—Bring them to me and get the people to recline.

They gathered in groups. Then Jesus took the loaves and the fish, looked up to heaven, blessed them and broke them.

Then he ordered his disciples to pass them among the crowd. Then some five thousand men, plus women and children ate bread and fish to their satisfaction. Afterwards they gathered twelve baskets full of leftovers.

(Jn. 6, 1-15; Mk. 6, 30-46)

Promise of the Eucharist

MANY of those who had eaten the miraculously multiplied bread, spent the night in the area surrounding the lake. They realized that the Apostles had left by boat, the only one they had brought, and that Jesus had stayed all by himself. Next day, together with some other people who came out by boat, they began to look for Jesus. They did not find him, so they went back to Capernaum by boat. When they found him, they asked him how he had come back.

Jesus began to advise them to be more concerned about the bread which came from heaven. They thought he was talking about the manna their ancestors ate in the desert. Jesus made it clear that those who ate manna had all died; but the bread he was talking about would give eternal life:

—I myself am the bread of life which comes from heaven; whoever eats this bread will live eternally. And the bread I will give, is my flesh, for the life of the world.

—How can he give us his flesh to eat? —they were murmuring among themselves.

Thereupon Jesus insisted:

—Amen, amen I say to you, if you do not eat the flesh of the Son of Man and drink his blood, you have no life in you; he who eats my flesh and drinks my blood, has eternal life and I will raise him on the last day.

After hearing these words many people broke away and did not follow him any more. Jesus then said to his Apostles:

—Do you want to leave me too?

—Lord, to whom shall we go? You have the words of eternal life. You are the Son of God —answered Peter.

(Jn. 6, 22-71)

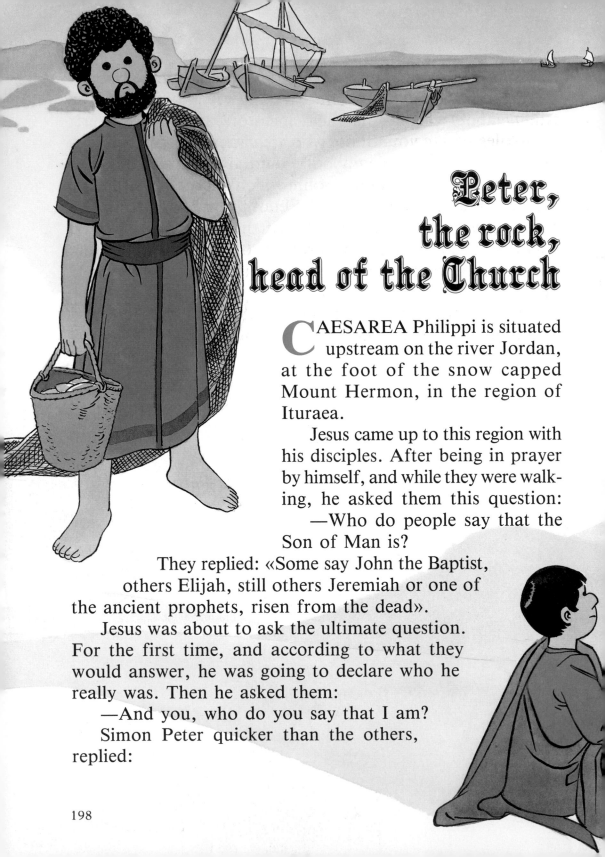

Peter, the rock, head of the Church

CAESAREA Philippi is situated upstream on the river Jordan, at the foot of the snow capped Mount Hermon, in the region of Ituraea.

Jesus came up to this region with his disciples. After being in prayer by himself, and while they were walking, he asked them this question:

—Who do people say that the Son of Man is?

They replied: «Some say John the Baptist, others Elijah, still others Jeremiah or one of the ancient prophets, risen from the dead».

Jesus was about to ask the ultimate question. For the first time, and according to what they would answer, he was going to declare who he really was. Then he asked them:

—And you, who do you say that I am?

Simon Peter quicker than the others, replied:

—You are the Christ, the Son of the living God.

Jesus did not correct Simon's answer; He accepted it as true and said to him:

—Blessed are you, Simon, for flesh and blood has not revealed this to you, but my Father in Heaven. And I say to you, you are Peter and upon this Rock I will build my Church, and the gates of hell shall not prevail against it. And I will give you the keys of the Kingdom of Heaven; and whatever you shall bind on earth, shall be bound in heaven, and whatever you shall loose on earth, shall be loosened in heaven.

When he finished saying this to Peter, he strictly charged his disciples to tell no one that he was Jesus the Christ.

(Mt. 16, 13-20)

The Transfiguration

MOUNT Tabor rises like an immense dome north of the plains of Jezreel, southeast of lake Tiberias; its peak elevated well above its surroundings, dominates an extensive view of the whole area.

It had been a few days since Jesus had announced to the Apostles his passion, death and resurrection. They did not understand anything about the cross; Peter even tried to convince the Master not to let these things happen to him.

Shortly afterwards Jesus took Peter, James and John up to the mountain. While in prayer, he was transfigured before their eyes. His face became as dazzling as the sun, his

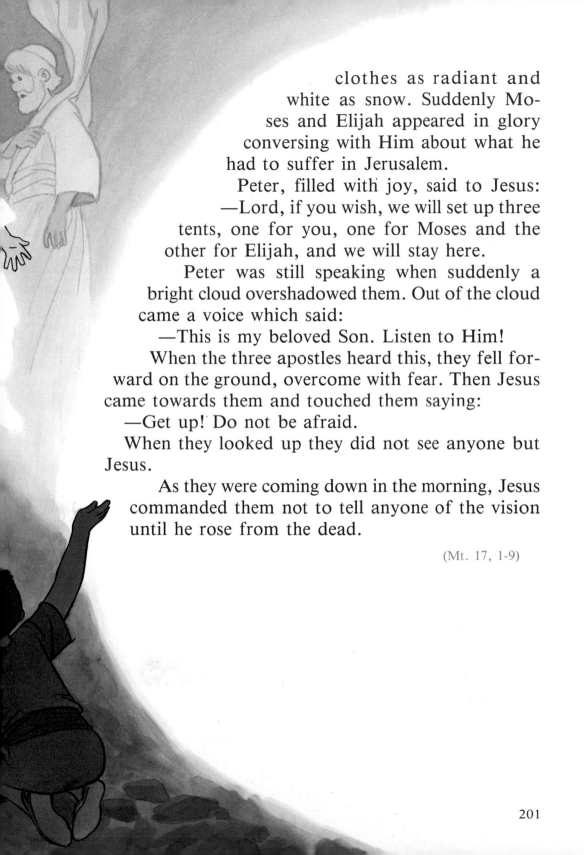

clothes as radiant and white as snow. Suddenly Moses and Elijah appeared in glory conversing with Him about what he had to suffer in Jerusalem.

Peter, filled with joy, said to Jesus:

—Lord, if you wish, we will set up three tents, one for you, one for Moses and the other for Elijah, and we will stay here.

Peter was still speaking when suddenly a bright cloud overshadowed them. Out of the cloud came a voice which said:

—This is my beloved Son. Listen to Him!

When the three apostles heard this, they fell forward on the ground, overcome with fear. Then Jesus came towards them and touched them saying:

—Get up! Do not be afraid.

When they looked up they did not see anyone but Jesus.

As they were coming down in the morning, Jesus commanded them not to tell anyone of the vision until he rose from the dead.

(Mt. 17, 1-9)

The man born blind

IT was some time since Jesus had left Galilee and he was walking through Judea. It was the last year of his life. As he walked along a street in Jerusalem, he saw a man who had been blind from birth. The Apostles asked him:

—Rabbi, who has sinned, this man or his parents, that he should be born blind?

—Neither of them. He was born blind so that the works of God were made manifest in him —Jesus answered. Then he spat on the ground and made clay with the spittle, and spread the clay over the blind man's eyes, and said to him:

—Go and wash in the pool of Siloe.

So he went away, and washed and returned seeing. The neighbours and the people who knew him, since they used to give him alms began to wonder if he was the one or somebody else who resembled him. But the man insisted that he was the blind one. In relation to this extraordinary matter they took him to the senate of the Jews.

He was interrogated, and he repeated once again: «He put clay upon my eyes, then I washed, and I see». The pharisees got involved in a discussion. Some said Jesus could not be a man of God because he had not kept the Sabbath, and that day was the Sabbath. The others said that if he was a sinner he could not perform such a miracle. So they decided that he had never been blind.

Jesus sought him out and asked him:

—Do you believe in the Son of God?

—Who is he, Lord, that I may believe in him?

—You have seen him; He is speaking to you now.

—I do believe, Lord!

(Jn. 9, 1-41)

The Lord's Prayer

JESUS was praying one day on the Mount of Olives, in the outskirts of Jerusalem; when he had finished, one of his disciples asked him:

—Lord, teach us to pray.

—When you pray, say: Our Father, who art in heaven, hallowed be thy name; thy kingdom come; thy will be done on earth as it is in heaven. Give us this day our daily bread; and forgive us our trespasses as we forgive those who trespass against us; and lead us not into temptation, but deliver us from evil.

He also said to them:

—If one of you has a friend, and he comes to your door at midnight asking for three loaves of bread for his supper, if your friend insists on knocking at the door, though you may be in bed, you will get up and give him what he needs, at least because you want him to leave you alone.

So I say to you: ask and you shall receive; seek and you shall find; knock and it shall be opened to you.

If a son asks you for bread, will you give him a stone?; or, if he asks for fish, will you give him a snake? If you, who are not good, know how to give your children good things, how much more will your heavenly Father give the Holy Spirit to those who ask him?

On another occasion Jesus said:

—Until now you haven't asked for anything in my name. Amen, Amen I say to you, anything you ask for in my name will be given to you.

(Lk. 11, 1-13; Jn. 14, 13-14)

The Prodigal Son

V ERY often Jesus was seen with tax collectors and sinners gathering around him, at which the pharisees gossiped. Then Jesus said to them:

—Not the healthy but the sick ones are in need of the physician. I have not come to seek the just ones but the sinners.

Then he addressed this parable to them:

—A man had two sons. The youngest one demanded his share of the state and the ability to dispose of it freely. So the father divided up the property, and the younger son, once he had converted his share into currency, went off to a distant land.

Being young and with money, he squandered all he had in dissolute living. His false friends contributed to his misery, to the extent he had to work on anything he could. He ended up taking care of pigs, but under such conditions he was even deprived of the husks that were fodder for the pigs.

Hunger and loneliness made him long for his father. He

would like to hug and to kiss him so much. But he didn't have any right to his love nor to his bread any more.

He thought he could be welcome, if not as a son, at least as one of the servants. He considered the words he would tell his father to show his sincere sorrow; then he set off on his way home.

His father saw him and ran out to meet him, he threw his arms around him and kissed him tearfully. The son began to say: «Father, I have sinned against God and against you; I no longer deserve to be called your son...». His father paid no attention to this, and said to his servants to bring the finest robe and sandals for his son, and to kill the fatted calf to celebrate that the son he thought was lost and dead, was back.

In the same way there will be joy in heaven for each sinner who repents —Jesus said.

(Lk. 15, 1-2; 11-32)

Resurrection of Lazarus

THE envy and conspiracies of scribes and pharisees were so many that they became a threat. So Jesus left Jerusalem and went to Bethany, as he had done on other occasions, to visit his friend Lazarus, who lived with his sisters Mary and Martha in this village, not too far from Jerusalem. Jesus went on his way to the valley of Jordan. It was here that he received a message:

—Lord, your friend Lazarus, whom you love so much, is sick.

—This sickness is not to end in death, rather it is for God's glory —Jesus said to his Apostles.

Two days afterwards Jesus said that they should return to Judea because Lazarus had died. They set off and, when they were near Bethany, Martha, who had heard that Jesus was coming, went to meet him; then she said to him:

—Lord, if you had been here my brother would never have died...

—Your brother will rise again —Jesus said.

Martha went back to tell her sister Mary that the teacher was there and was asking for her. The Jews who had come from Jerusalem to console them and were in the house, thought she was going to the tomb, and followed her. When Mary came to the place where Jesus was, she fell at his feet in tears, groaning like her sister before. Jesus was troubled in spirit and began to weep.

—Where have you laid him? —He asked.

—Lord, come and see.

When they approached the tomb, Jesus directed them to remove the stone which was laid against the entrance. Martha warned him about the stench, for it was four days since Lazarus had died. Jesus looked upwards to heaven in prayer; then he called loudly:

—Lazarus, come out!

At once he came out and stood before the tomb.

(Jn. 11, 1-44)

Jesus and the children

ONE time, when they arrived at the house where they were staying, some mothers brought their children for Jesus to touch them, lay his hands on them and pray for them.

The Apostles intervened, removing the children and scolding the mothers for bothering the Teacher with those kids.

When Jesus noticed this, he called the children and reprimanded the Apostles:

　—Let the children come to me and do not shut them off.
The reign of God is theirs and of those who become like them.
　Then Jesus put his arms around them and played with them.

(Mk. 9, 33-37; Lk. 18, 15-17)

211

The rich young man

JESUS was leaving a town to continue on his way, when a young man, who belonged to a rich family, came running to meet him and asked him:

—Teacher, what good must I do to possess everlasting life?

—Keep the Commandments —Jesus answered, and went on—: You know them already: You shall not kill; you shall not bear false witness; honour your father and your mother, and love your neighbour as yourself.

—I have kept them since childhood. What else can I do?

Jesus smiled, looked at him and said:

—There is one thing further you must do: if you seek perfection, go, sell your possessions and give to the poor; you will then have a treasure in heaven. Afterward come back and follow me.

The young man had many possessions and, upon hearing this he went away sad. Then Jesus said to his disciples:

—How difficult it is for a rich man to enter into the kingdom of heaven!

The disciples were overwhelmed by the Teacher's words; but Jesus insisted:

—My children, I say to you again: How difficult it is to enter into the kingdom of heaven for those who have placed their trust in money! It is easier for a camel to pass through the eye of a needle.

—Then, who can be saved? —the disciples exclaimed. Then it was Peter who asked:

—What is going to happen to us who have left everything we had to follow you?

—You and all those who have given up parents, wife, brothers, children, home and for my sake and for the Gospel's sake, will receive many times as much, together with persecutions in this life, and will inherit everlasting life —Jesus answered them.

(Mt. 19, 23-30; Lk. 18, 24-30)

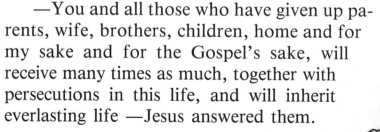

Zacchaeus

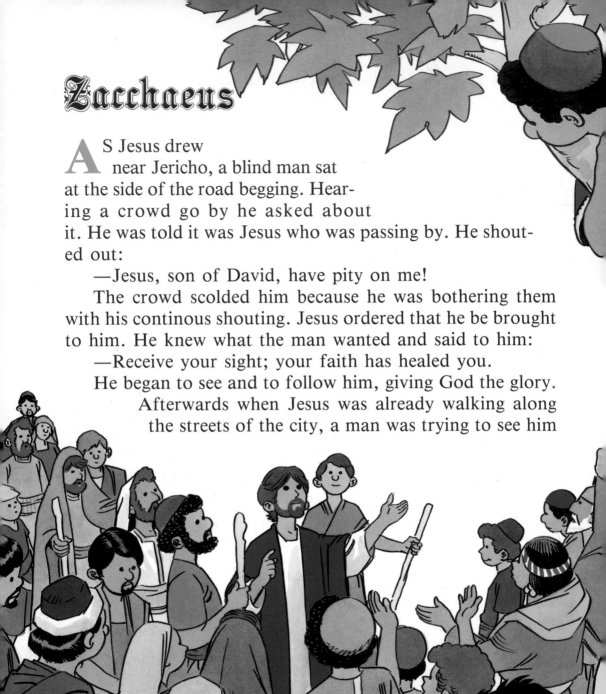

AS Jesus drew near Jericho, a blind man sat at the side of the road begging. Hearing a crowd go by he asked about it. He was told it was Jesus who was passing by. He shouted out:

—Jesus, son of David, have pity on me!

The crowd scolded him because he was bothering them with his continous shouting. Jesus ordered that he be brought to him. He knew what the man wanted and said to him:

—Receive your sight; your faith has healed you.

He began to see and to follow him, giving God the glory.

Afterwards when Jesus was already walking along the streets of the city, a man was trying to see him

because he had heard a lot about Jesus and He wanted to know him. This man was called Zacchaeus; he was rich and chief of the tax collectors, known as publicans and considered sinners. Zacchaeus, being small of stature, was unable to see Jesus because of the crowd; he first ran on in front, then he climbed a sycamore tree which was along the Teacher's route in order to see him.

When Jesus came to the spot he looked up and saw Zacchaeus. They looked at each other, and Jesus said.

—Zacchaeus, hurry down! I mean to stay at your house today.

Many people began to murmur because he had gone to a sinner's house.

When they had finished their meal Zacchaeus said to Jesus:

—Lord, I give half my belongings to the poor. If I have defrauded anyone in the least, I will pay him back fourfold.

Jesus said to him:

—Today salvation has come to this house.

(Lk. 18, 35-43; 19, 1-10)

Jesus returns to Bethany

SIX days before the Passover, Jesus returned to Bethany, on his way to Jerusalem, to celebrate this feast. There they gave him a banquet at the house of Simon the leper. Martha waited on them, and Lazarus, whom Jesus had raised from the dead, was also at the table. Mary brought an alabaster jar with a pound of perfume made from aromatic nard.

As Jesus was at the table she anointed his feet with the perfume; then she broke the jar and poured what was left over his head, and the house was filled with the ointment's fragrance.

Judas Iscariot, the one about to hand him over, said:

—What is the point of this waste?

Jesus came up to defend her with these words:

M. Querada

—Leave her alone, for the poor you will always have with you, and you can help them whenever you want, but will not always have me. For in pouring this ointment on my body, she has done it for my burial. I assure you, wherever the Gospel is proclaimed, throughout the world, what she did will be spoken of as her memorial.

(Jn. 12, 1-11; Mt. 26, 6-13)

Triumphal entry into Jerusalem

JESUS rested on the Sabbath in Bethany. Next morning he went on his way up to Jerusalem and began to ascend the slope east of the Mount of Olives. Jesus asked that a donkey be brought to him. They laid their clothes on the beast and Jesus mounted. The crowd, who had gathered to celebrate the Passover, began to cry out:

—Hosanna to the Son of David!

Many people removed their cloaks and spread them on the road as Jesus was passing by; others cut branches from the olive trees and laid them along his path. When Jerusalem was in sight and they began to descend, the shouting grew:

—Blessed is the King who comes in the name of the Lord! Hosanna in the highest!

Some pharisees said to Jesus:

—Teacher, reprimand your disciples.

—I say to you; if these people become silent, the stones will shout.

Then Jesus, contemplating Jerusalem, wept for it. In the meantime, news spread out all over that Jesus was arriving, and a large crowd came out of the city to meet him, waving palms and branches of olive trees and acclaiming him.

This is how Jesus entered through the streets of Jerusalem, and how the whole city was stirred up. Then he entered the temple and cured the sick who were brought to him. The children, moved by the enthusiasm, also began to shout:

—Hosanna to the Son of David!

(Mt. 21, 1-17; Jn. 12, 12-19)

Washing of the feet

JESUS came up again to Jerusalem. Thursday was the first day of the Passover, and the Apostles asked him:

—Where do you wish us to go to prepare the Passover supper for you?

Jesus sent Peter and John, saying to them:

—Go into the city and you will come upon a man carrying a water jar; follow him and whatever house he enters, say to the owner that you are my envoys. Get everything ready for me.

Once in the cenacle they reclined at table, and he said to them:

—I have greatly desired to eat this Passover with you before I suffer.

During the meal Jesus stood up, took off his cloak, and tied a towel around himself. Then he poured water into a basin and began to wash his disciples' feet and dry them with the towel. Thus he came to Peter, who refused:

—You shall never wash my feet!

—Then, you will have no share in my heritage.

—Lord, then not only my feet, but my hands and head as well.

—The man who is clean has no need to wash except for his feet, just as you are; though not all.

He said this on account of Judas. When he had finished he said to them:

—I have given you an example: as I have done, so you must do to others.

(Mk. 14, 12-17; Jn. 13, 1-17)

The betrayer

O N Tuesday night there was an urgent meeting in the courtyard of the High Priest Caiaphas' palace: they agreed
on destroying Jesus, but only after the Holy Days were over
to prevent people from revolting against them.

This happened about the same hour that Jesus was telling
his Apostles that within two days the Son of Man would be

crucified. Judas Iscariot was not with them because he had gone to talk to the chief priests:

—Tell me how much you will pay me and I will hand him over to you...

Upon hearing this they were jubilant and promised to give him thirty silver coins. They agreed; Judas for his part would look for the opportunity to hand Jesus over.

During the Last Supper, after the washing of the feet, Jesus, who was deeply troubled, said:

—Amen, amen, I say to you, one of you will betray me.

—Lord, who is he? —they asked.

—For one of the twelve who is eating with me, better if he had never been born.

John was close to Jesus and leaned back against his chest; then he asked who was the one. Jesus answered very softly: «The one to whom I give the bit of food I dip in the dish».

No sooner had Judas eaten the morsel than he stood up to go out. Jesus said to him:

—Be quick about what you are to do.

Shortly after his betrayal, Judas flung the coins away and hanged himself.

(Mt. 26, 1-5; Jn. 13, 18-21; Mt. 27, 3-10)

The Last Supper

AFTER Judas had left the cenacle Jesus said:
—Now is the Son of Man glorified, and God is glorified in him. My children, I am not to be with you much longer.

When the supper was ended, Jesus took bread, gave thanks, blessed and broke it and gave it to them saying:

—Take this, all of you, and eat it: this is my body which will be given up for you.

Then he took the cup with the wine; again he gave thanks and blessed and gave it, saying:

—Take this all of you, and drink from it: this is the cup of my blood, the blood of the new and everlasting Covenant. It will be shed for many so that sins may be forgiven. Do this in memory of me.

Jesus also gave them a new commandment:

—Love one another as I have loved you.

To Peter, who had boasted he would follow him even to death, he said that before the cock crowed he would disown him three times. Then, looking up to heaven, he prayed, saying:

—Father, the hour has come. I have made your name known to men, so they may have eternal life. For these you have given me I pray, and for those who will believe in me through their word. That your love for me lives in them.

(Mt. 26, 26-35; Jn. 14-17)

In the Garden of Gethsemani

AFTER leaving the cenacle, Jesus and the Apostles went to the garden of olives. He took Peter, James and John with him, and left the others at the garden's entrance. Then he said:

—My soul is sad; wait here and watch with me.

He went forward a little, and fell prostrated down to the ground. And this was his prayer:

—My Father, if it is possible, let this cup pass away from me; yet let it be as you would have it, not as I.

He remained in prayer for a long while. Twice he returned to his disciples and he found them asleep. He was deeply hurt and reprimanded them because they didn't stay awake in prayer with him, in those moments of profound sadness. While in prayer, his anguish was so intense that he sweated drops of blood. He came out comforted after praying and ready to face everything that was coming to him. In the silence of the night, Jesus heard the steps of the crowd getting close; then, he woke up his Apostles:

—Get up! My betrayer is here.

Judas had arranged with the chief priests and elders of the people to give them a signal:

—The man I shall kiss is the one; take hold of him.

And he went over to Jesus and kissed him.

—Friend, would you betray the Son of Man with a kiss? —Jesus said to Judas; and then, he asked the crowd:

—Who is it you want?

—Jesus the Nazorean —they answered.

—I am He; but if I am the one you want, let these men go.

With that the Apostles fled and Jesus let himself be arrested.

(Jn. 18, 1-12;
Mt. 26, 36-56)

Jesus before Annas and Caiaphas

THE old man Annas had been a High Priest. He was a cunning manipulator of intrigues, and he got his son-in-law Caiaphas to be his successor. They took Jesus to him first.

Annas interrogated Jesus about his disciples and doctrine. Jesus simply answered:

—I have always spoken publicly. Why do you question me? Question those who have heard me; they will know what I said.

Annas next sent him to Caiaphas, who was assembled with the members of his senate who were expecting Jesus.

Annas stood up and solemnly said to him:

—I order you to tell us under oath if you are the Son of God.

—It is I. And I tell you this: soon you will see the Son of Man seated at the right hand of the Almighty God, and coming on the clouds of Heaven.

At this Caiaphas tore his robes, and said:

—You have heard it. He has blasphemed! What is your verdict?

—He deserves death —was the assembly's sentence.

(Jn. 18, 13-14, 19-24; Mt. 26, 57, 59-68)

Peter's denial

PETER and another disciple followed Jesus at a prudent distance, all the way from Gethsemany to the palace of Annas and Caiaphas. Peter remained at the door, and the other, known to the servants, was allowed to go in. But he came out and spoke to the woman at the gate, and then brought Peter in. The courtyard was rather large and porched; Annas' residence was at one side and Caiaphas' at the other; in the center the guards had made a bonfire to protect themselves from the cold of the night.

The girl gate keeper looked at Peter and asked him:

—Are you not one of this man's followers?

—No, I am not —Peter quickly answered.

He sat down under the porch, when another servant noticed him:

—This man used to be with Jesus the Nazorean.

—I don't know that man —Peter swore.

Peter then joined those who wcre near the fire warming themselves. One of them looked at him and asked him:

—Aren't you a disciple of his?

—I don't know what you are talking about, I am not!

After a while another said:

—He surely is a follower of Jesus; you can tell he is a Galilean.

Peter began to curse, and to swear:

—I do not even know the man you are talking about!

—I saw you with him in the garden —another assured him.

Peter denied it once again. At that moment a cock crowed. Jesus was passing by across the courtyard after his trial before Caiaphas, and looked at Peter. He remembered the words Jesus had said earlier, and went out and wept bitterly.

(Jn. 18, 15-18; Mk. 14, 66-72)

Jesus before Pilate

THE sentence dictated by the Jewish court had to be revised and executed by the Roman governor Pontius Pilate. At daybreak they brought Jesus to the praetorium where Pilate listened to the accusations. He was accused of subverting the people, opposing the payment of taxes to Caesar, and calling himself the Christ, a King.

Pilate then interrogated Jesus about these accusations. To the question about if he was a king, Jesus answered:

—I am a king, but my kingdom does not belong to this world.

The governor knew he was innocent, and said so. But the crowd came out to demand the pardon it was customary to give at Passover. Pilate gave them the option to choose between a murderer called Barabbas and Jesus. The chief priests instigated the crowd to cry out:

—Away with this man: release Barabbas for us!

—What shall I do with Jesus, who is called the Christ!

—Crucify him, crucify him!

—I have not found anything about him that calls for death; I will therefore chastise him and release him.

—Crucify him, crucify him!

Pilate then decreed to release Barabbas and that Jesus be scourged. In the courtyard he was stripped and tortured by scourging; they wove a crown of thorns and fixed it on his head; they put a cloak of royal purple around his shoulders and then they stuck a reed in his hands like a sceptre. Pilate showed him to the people:

—Behold, the man!

—Crucify him! According to our law he must die because he calls himself the Son of God.

Pilate gave in; he washed his hands before the people saying: «I am innocent of the blood of this just man». Then he handed him over to be crucified.

(Jn. 18, 28-40; 19, 1-16; Lk. 23, 1-25)

Death upon the cross

RIGHT after Pilate's co-
wardly decision, they
dressed Jesus in his own
clothes; then he carried the
cross by himself. And, guarded by Roman
soldiers, Jesus went out to what is called
Calvary, on the outskirts of the city.

The centurion laid hold of a farmer called Simon the Cyrenean to help Jesus to
carry the crossbeam, for it was very heavy.

It was midday when they arrived. After stripping him, they nailed his hands and feet to the cross. With Jesus they crucified two thieves, one on his right hand and one on his left.

The soldiers readied themselves to wait for Jesus to die. Jesus in his agony prayed:

—Father, forgive them, for they do not know what they are doing.

One of the thieves asked him:

—Lord, remember me when you enter into your kingdom.

—I assure you: this day you will be with me in paradise.

Near the cross stood his mother and his disciple John. And Jesus said:

—Woman, there is your son. —And to the disciple:— There is your mother.

It was now the midafternoon. Darkness came over the land. Jesus uttered a loud cry and said:

—Father, into your hands I commend my spirit.

And bowing his head, he expired. The earth quaked, and the curtain of the sanctuary was torn in two.

(Jn. 19, 17-30; Lk. 23, 26-46)

The burial

WHEN the centurion saw the manner of Jesus' death and the phenomena that happened, he said:

—Clearly this was the Son of God.

And the crowd, which had gathered over there watched horrified at what had happened, went home beating their breasts.

One of the soldiers thrust a lance into Jesus' side to be sure that he was dead.

Joseph of Arimathea, an upright and holy man, and an illustrious senator, who had not been associated with the decisions taken against Jesus, approached Pilate with a request for Jesus' body. He went to Calvary carrying a fine linen shroud he had bought. Nicodemus likewise came, bringing a mixture of myrrh and aloes, which weighed about one hundred pounds, to embalm the body. Both were Jesus' disciples, but in secret.

It was sunset and the time of rest

was getting near to start
keeping the Sabbath of the Passover. They took the body of Jesus, washed
it, anointed it and wrapped it in the shroud.
Joseph had a new tomb hewn from a rock. They laid
Jesus in it and rolled the stone, prepared to close the entrance.

A group of women, among them Mary the mother of Jesus
and Mary Magdalene, returned to Jerusalem and bought aromas and ointments to bury Jesus with dignity, when the Sabbath of Passover was over.

The elders of the Jesus, still shaken by the things that had
happened at Jesus' death, went to Pilate to request that soldiers be assigned to keep the tomb under surveillance, after
fixing a seal to the stone.

(Mt. 27, 57-66; Jn. 19, 38-42)

The Resurrection

A T daybreak of the first day of the week, the soldiers felt a strong tremor under their feet and brightness of lightning which scared them. Terrified, they ran to tell what had happened.

About the same time the group of women came out of the house with ointments and aromas. They were saying to one another: «Who will roll back the stone for us from the tomb». When they got near, they found that the stone had been rolled back. On entering the tomb they realized that Jesus' body wasn't there, straight away Mary Magdalene ran to inform Peter and John of the news. The rest of the women remained there; then they saw a young man sitting at the right, dressed in a white robe, who said to them.

—Do not be terrified. You are looking for Jesus of Nazareth. He has risen, he is not here. Go and tell his disciples.

238

Peter and John ran to the tomb and verified what they were told by Mary Magdalene, who also was running after them. John believed that Jesus had risen when he saw the linen the body of Jesus had been wrapped with. They both returned to the city. Mary Magdalene remained outside weeping at the tomb; she saw a man standing by and thinking he was the gardener, said to him:

—Sir, if you have removed him, tell me where you have laid him.

—Mary! —Jesus said.

—Teacher! —she exclaimed on recognizing him. She fell to her knees and embraced his feet.

Jesus also appeared to the group of women as they were walking into town:

—Peace! Go and bring the news to my brothers that they are to go to Galilee where they will see me.

When the women recognized Jesus, they worshiped him.

(Mk. 16, 1-11; Mt. 28, 1-15; Jn. 20, 1-18)

Emmaus

TWO of the disciples that same morning were making their way to a village named Emmaus, seven miles distant from Jerusalem, discussing as they went all these things that had happened.

At a crossroads some unknown man approached and asked them:

—What words are these that you are exchanging, and why are you so sad?

—Are you the only one who does not know the things that have happened these past days?

—What things? —the newcomer asked.

—All those things had to do with Jesus of Nazareth —one of them answered.

After telling everything they did to him, he said:

—We were hoping that he was the one to set Israel free, but... It's true that some women have scared us this morning as they told us they had some visions, and some of our men went to the tomb and found it empty; but him they did not see.

The newcomer said to them:

—How slow you are to believe! Isn't it written that the Christ had to suffer these things before entering into his glory?

And beginning then with Moses and all the prophets, he interpreted to them all the things they had said about the Messiah.

And they drew near the house. The man acted as though he was going on, but they urged him to stay with them, because it was getting late. And he went in with them. When they reclined at the table he took bread, pronounced the blessing, broke the bread and began to distribute it to them. With that their eyes were opened and they recognized Jesus; whereupon he vanished from their sight.

They got up immediately and, full of joy, they returned to Jerusalem to tell the group what had happened to them.

(Lk. 24, 13-35)

Jesus appears to the Apostles

THE disciples from Emmaus found the group locked in the cenacle, for they were afraid of the Jews. Peter affirmed that Jesus had risen and had appeared to him; the two men from Emmaus recounted how they had recognized him at the breaking of bread. The others found themselves between the fear that such a thing wasn't true and the joy that it might

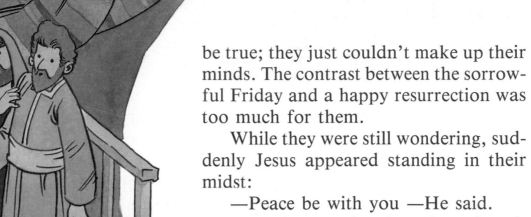

be true; they just couldn't make up their minds. The contrast between the sorrowful Friday and a happy resurrection was too much for them.

While they were still wondering, suddenly Jesus appeared standing in their midst:

—Peace be with you —He said.

—Look at my hands and my feet; it is really I; touch and see that a ghost does not have flesh and bones as I do.

He showed them his wounded hands and feet and his side. They were still incredulous for sheer joy and wonder that they were seeing the Lord.

Then He breathed on them and said:

—As the Father has sent me, so I send you. Receive the Holy Spirit. If you forgive men's sins they are forgiven them; if you hold them bound, they are held bound. Peace be with you.

(Jn. 20, 19-24; Lk. 24, 36-45)

By the sea of Tiberias

AS Jesus had indicated, the Apostles went from Jerusalem to the region of Galilee. One evening they went to fish out in the lake of Tiberias in Peter's boat. They came back at daybreak; all through the night they caught nothing.

From the shore someone asked:

—Have you caught anything?

—Not a thing —they answered.

—Cast your net to the right and you will find something.

They cast therefore, and now they were unable to draw it up for the great number of fishes. John said it was the Lord. On hearing it, Peter jumped into the water and swam to the shore.

—Bring some of the fish, and come and eat —Jesus said to them.

When they had eaten their meal, Jesus said to Peter:

—Simon, son of John, do you love me more than these?

—Yes, Lord, you know that I love you —Peter said.

—Feed my lambs —Jesus said.

A second time he asked him the same question, and Peter gave the same answer. Jesus replied:

—Tend my sheep.

A third time Jesus asked him:

—Simon, son of John, do you love me?

Peter was grieved because he had asked the same question for the third time.

—Lord, you know everything; you know that I love you.

—Feed my sheep —Jesus said again. Then he added: Follow me!

(Jn. 21, 1-19)

The Ascension

FOR forty days after his resurrection, Jesus instructed the Apostles about the kingdom of God.

After appearing to them on several occasions, he told them to go back to Jerusalem. And being with them at the table in the cenacle, He told them not to leave Jerusalem, because:

—In a few days you will receive the power of the Holy Spirit; then you are to be my witnesses in Jerusalem, in Judea, yes, even to the ends of the earth.

Then he led them out of the city, to the top of the mount of Olives near Bethany, and with hands upraised, blessed them. No sooner had he blessed them when he was lifted up before their eyes in a cloud which took him from their sight. The Apostles gazed up into the heaven's seeing him disappear.

Two men dressed in white robes said to them:

—Men of Galilee, why do you stand here looking up at the skies? This Jesus will return, just as you saw him go up into the heavens.

After that they returned full of joy to the city. They remained in the cenacle, where they were staying, together with Mary the mother of Jesus, in expectation of the promised Holy Spirit.

At one point during those days, Peter proposed to elect a man to take the place of Judas Iscariot. He would have to be a witness of the life of Jesus, from the baptism of John to the resurrection and ascension. Of the one hundred and twenty disciples gathered together there were two who qualified. They prayed and drew lots: the choice fell to Mathias; and so the number of the twelve Apostles was completed.

(Lk. 24, 50-52; Acts 1, 1-26)

Descent of the Holy Spirit

FIFTY days after Passover, the Jews celebrated the feast of Pentecost. They came from every nation to the temple of Jerusalem to thank God for the harvest, and also to commemorate rate the revelation of the Law of God at Mount Sinai.

Ten days after the ascension of Jesus, the day of Pentecost,

the Apostles gathered together in the cenacle. Suddenly from up in the sky there came a noise like a strong driving wind which shook the whole house. Tongues as of fire appeared, which parted and came to rest on each of them. All were filled with Holy Spirit; and began to speak in different tongues.

On hearing such a noise, a large crowd assembled in front of the house where the Apostles were staying. On account of the feast, there were many devout Jews in Jerusalem who came from many nations: from Greece, Rome, Mesopotamia, Cappadocia, Egypt, Lybia... They were dumbfounded and they asked one another:

—Are not all of these men Galileans? How is it that each of us hears them in his native tongue? What does this mean?

(Acts 2, 1-41)

The Church keeps growing

THE number of believers kept growing. They gathered together in different houses to celebrate the Eucharist, and helped each other with their goods.

The Apostles, with great courage, gave testimony to the resurrection of the Lord Jesus, and announced everything that He had commanded them. They performed many wonders and signs among the people.

Once, when Peter and John were going up to the temple for prayer in the afternoon and about to enter through the gate called «The Beautiful», a man crippled from birth, who used to beg from people every day, stretched his hand out expecting some coins from them. Peter fixed his gaze on the man, and said:

—I have neither silver nor gold, but what I have I give you; in the name of Jesus Christ, stand up and walk.

He jumped up and went into the temple with them, jumping about and praising God. The crippled man was very well known, so the people were struck with astonishment at what had happened to him.

The Apostles were jailed several times. On one occasion Gamaliel said to the other members of the senate:

—Leave these men alone because, if what they teach is the work of men, it will destroy itself; but if it comes from God, you will not be able to destroy it.

In spite of it, however, they had them whipped and then they let them free, but ordered them not to speak about Jesus anymore. Peter replied:

—You had better judge by yourselves if we are more obliged to obey men than God.

After this they left full of joy that they had suffered whipping for Jesus' sake.

(Acts 3; 4, 1-37; 5, 12-42)

The first martyr

THE Apostles needed more time to dedicate themselves to prayer and to the word. They put their hands over seven men and they called them deacons, to be their helpers. One of these deacons was Stephen.

Some Jews belonging to the synagogue of Jerusalem, began to debate with Stephen; but they couldn't refute his reasons and the spirit with which he spoke. Then they incited the people. All together they seized him and led him off to the Sanhedrin. After some false witnesses had testified, the High Priest asked him:

—Is it true everything they say against you? Stephen took the floor and gave a long talk going over the history of Israel, recalling the moments when it rebelled against God and against his messengers.

He finished thus:

—You stiff, necked people! As your fathers did before, you are opposing the Holy Spirit. They put to death those who foretold the coming of the Just One, and you, in your turn have become his betrayers and murderers.

Those who listened to his words were stung to the heart. Stephen meanwhile looked at the sky and exclaimed:

—I see an opening in the sky, and the Son of Man standing at God's right hand.

The onlookers, shouting aloud and holding their hands over their ears, rushed at him and dragged him out of the city to stone him. As Stephen was being stoned he prayed thus:

—Lord Jesus, do not hold this sin against them.

That day saw the beginning of a great persecution of the Church in Jerusalem. All except the Apostles scattered throughout the countryside of Judea and Samaria.

And this dispersion marked the beginning of the expansion of the Gospel.

(Acts 6, 8-15; 7; 8, 1-4)

Saul's conversion

A young man called Saul was taking care of the cloaks of those who stoned Stephen. He was from Tarsus in Cilicia. He got letters from the High Priest who empowered him to arrest all the disciples he could find, and bring them to Jerusalem. And he set off for Damascus. As he traveled along

and was approaching the city, a light from the sky suddenly flashed about him. He fell to the ground and at the same time he heard a voice saying:

—Saul, Saul, why do you persecute me?

—Who are you, Sir?

—I am Jesus, the one you are persecuting. Get up and go into the city, where you will be told what to do.

Saul got up from the ground unable to see, even though his eyes were open. They had to take him by the hand and lead him into Damascus. Within three days he was baptized, and regained his sight.

He soon began to proclaim in the synagogues that Jesus was the Son of God. When the Jews saw that his conversion was sincere, they conspired to kill him as a traitor.

In order to save his life, the brethren took him to the harbour where he embarked to go to his home town Tarsus.

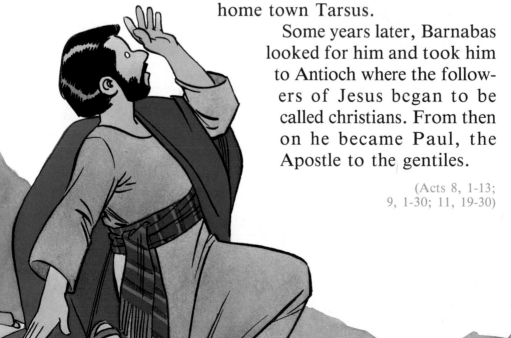

Some years later, Barnabas looked for him and took him to Antioch where the followers of Jesus began to be called christians. From then on he became Paul, the Apostle to the gentiles.

(Acts 8, 1-13;
9, 1-30; 11, 19-30)

Maps

EXODUS
OF THE
JEWISH PEOPLE

MEDITERRANEAN SEA

BASHAN

Death of Moses

CANAAN

AMMOM

Canaan explorers

Dibon-Gad

DEAD SEA

MOAB

Hormah

THE SINAI
PENINSULA

Baal-Zephon

Kadesh Barne

The bronze
serpent

Crossing of
the Red Sea

Oboth

Succoth

Column of fire

Etham

Rain of Manna

Punon

EDOM

NILE RIVER

Marah

Death of Aaron

Flood
of water

The burning bush

Elah

Dophkah

ARABIAN DESERT

Alush

Rafidim

Hazeroth

Tabera

ARABIA

SEA OF REEDS

SEA OF REEDS

Tablets of
the Law

EGYPT

RED SEA

259

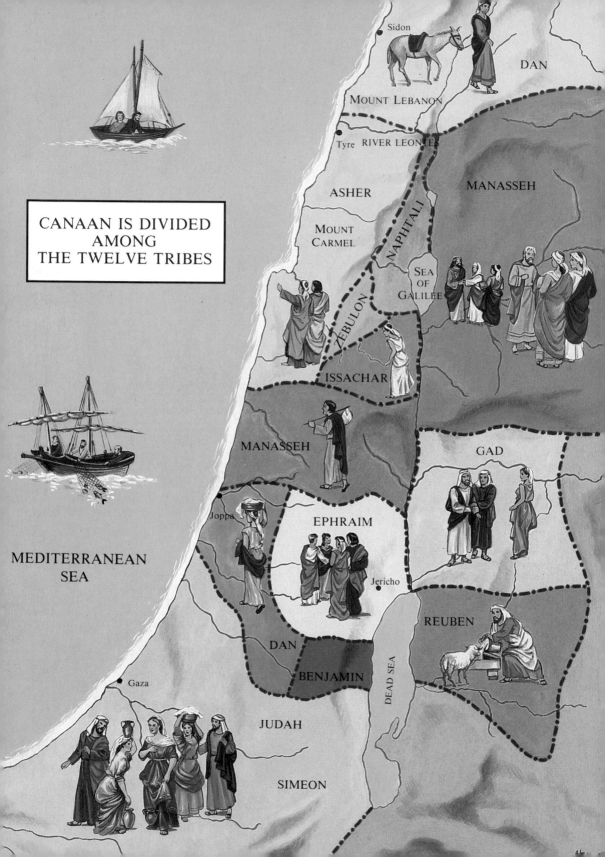

CANAAN IS DIVIDED
AMONG
THE TWELVE TRIBES

MEDITERRANEAN
SEA

Sidon

MOUNT LEBANON

DAN

Tyre RIVER LEONTES

ASHER

MANASSEH

MOUNT
CARMEL

ZEBULON

SEA
OF
GALILEE

NAPHTALI

ISSACHAR

MANASSEH

GAD

Joppa

EPHRAIM

Jericho

REUBEN

DAN

BENJAMIN

DEAD SEA

Gaza

JUDAH

SIMEON

PALESTINE
AT THE TIME
OF CHRIST

MYSIA

ITALY

ADRIATIC SEA

ILLYRIA

MACEDONIA

Rome

Three Taverns

pii Forum

Puteoli

TYRRHENIAN
SEA

SICILY

Messina

Rhegium

Syracuse

MALTA

EPIRUS

Philippi

Neapolis

Amphipolis

Thessalonica

Apollonia

Berdea

ACHAIA

Athens

Corinth

Cenchreae

CYRENAICA

APOSTOLIC JOURNEYS OF ST. PAUL

FIRST JOURNEY:

SECOND JOURNEY:

THIRD JOURNEY:

FORTH JOURNEY: